17

-4. MAR

21. D

Sep
23.
23.

18.

By the same author

A Mentally Handicapped Child in the Family
Away from Home: The Mentally Handicapped in Residential Care

Mary McCormack

The generation gap
The view from both sides

Constable · London

First published in Great Britain 1985
by Constable and Company Limited
10 Orange Street, London WC2H 7EG
Copyright © 1985 by Mary McCormack
Set in Linotron Times 10 pt by
Rowland Phototypesetting Limited
Bury St Edmunds, Suffolk
Printed in Great Britain by
St Edmundsbury Press
Bury St Edmunds, Suffolk

British Library CIP data

McCormack, Mary
The generation gap: the view from both sides
1. Adolescence   2. Parent and child
I. Title
306.8′7   HQ796

ISBN 0 09 465660 6
ISBN 0 09 466340 8 Pbk

Acknowledgements

I should like to thank the following for their help: Moira Hamlin, Darwin Shreve, Sheila Schüler, Peggy Wakelin, Dr Edna Irwin, Dr George Cohen, Joan Goode, Bob Belding, Mike Carr, Cynthia Leonard, Keith Chadwick, Sue Fallon, Jean Way, Lilian Grant and Laurence Gordon who took time to talk to me from their professional viewpoint.

I am grateful too to the groups, schools, colleges, work-places and invididuals who co-operated with the exercise; and last – but certainly not least – to the parents and the teenagers who agreed to be interviewed

I should like to thank the following for use of short quotations from their books: Barrie & Jenkins Ltd for Carson McCullers' *Member of the Wedding*; Alison Lurie and William Heinemann Ltd for *The War between the Tates*; John Conger and Harper & Row Inc., for *Adolescents – Generation under Pressure*; Irma Kurtz and Ebury Press for *Crisis – A Guide to your Emotions*; James Hemming and Ebury Press for *You and your Adolescent*, Carol Lee and the Writers and Readers Cooperative Society for *The Ostrich Position*; Laurie Lee and The Hogarth Press for *Cider with Rosie*; Clare Rayner for *Related to Sex* and Miriam Stoppard and Victor Gollancz Ltd for *Talking Sex*.

M.McC.
January 1985

Contents

PART ONE

Adolescents

1

Is adolescence really necessary?

'There was none of this adolescence nonsense when I
was a lad. No time for it. We were too busy working,
trying to earn a few shillings, to worry about disagreeing
with our parents. And they had their hands full, keeping
the younger ones clothed and fed. There wasn't time for
adolescence if you ask me.'

68-year-old grandfather of one of the
teenage interviewees

Teenagers, as a tribe, a culture and a multi-million pound industry,
were invented sometime in the 1950s, but adolescence and its
problems have been with us much longer – whatever the grandfather quoted above believes. Perhaps, because childhood was
foreshortened by work and because families were larger and more
time-consuming in the past, people didn't have time to notice it so
acutely.

The Greeks may not have had a word for it, but they certainly
knew the condition. In the year 400 BC, Socrates was writing: 'They
have bad manners and contempt for authority. They are ready to
contradict their parents, monopolise conversation in company, eat
gluttonously and tyrannise their teachers.' He was writing about
adolescents.

Anna Freud, following in her father's footsteps, was putting it
even more strongly by the 1950s: 'Adolescence is by its nature an
interruption of peaceful growth, and . . . the upholding of a steady
equilibrium during the adolescent process is in itself abnormal. The
adolescent manifestations come close to symptoms of the neurotic,
psychotic or dissocial order and merge almost imperceptibly into
. . . almost all the mental illnesses.'

The person usually attributed with pinpointing adolescence as a
separate and stormy segment of all our lives was the French
philosopher, Jean-Jacques Rousseau, in the second half of the
eighteenth century.

'Man is not meant to remain a child for ever. At the time
prescribed by nature he passes out of his childhood. As the fretting
of the sea precedes the distant storm, this disturbing change is

announced by the murmur of nascent passions. A change of mood, frequent tantrums, a constant unease of mind makes the child hard to manage. He no longer listens to his master's voice. He mistrusts his guide and is averse to control.'

Philosophy is one thing; real life on the factory floor often quite another. But by early and mid-nineteenth century, the law had come round to the same view as Rousseau. Two factory acts protected young people between 13 and 18 from the full rigours of factory life, and the Youthful Offenders Act meant that they were treated differently from the mature law-breaker.

So the adolescent, that exotic creature teetering between childhood and adulthood, and failing to fit comfortably into either camp, was officially with us.

The generation gap, that cavern of misunderstanding and aggravation between parent and child, has probably been a part of life since Adam and Eve had a spot of bother with their two lads.

Odd really, when you think about it. We all make the difficult journey through adolescence. We all know what it feels like. You'd think then that first-hand experience would have made parents experts at understanding their own children's feelings and difficulties, when their turn comes.

Far from it. By the time parents have children in or approaching their teens, they have either forgotten what it was like to be that age, they have tinted the memory with the rosy nostalgia, or the rules have totally changed.

So the struggle starts from scratch each time: the struggle for independence on the one side; for the right to control, direct and guide on the other.

There is, however, an encouraging modern line of enquiry, which suggests that maybe the psychologists and sociologists have exaggerated the generation gap over the years. Instigator of this theory is the highly-respected Michael Rutter. In the 1970s, he posed the question 'Adolescent turmoil – fact or fiction?' – and set out to answer it by way of a study of 14 and 15-year-olds on the Isle of Wight.

His conclusions contrast with what other observers have been saying for centuries. Were they only observing the minority of seriously disturbed cases, he wonders? Rutter found that, whilst parent–child disagreement over everyday items like clothes and hair are frequent, 'parent–child alienation' was not common.

According to his sample of parents, only a small number of 14-year-olds withdrew from involvement with the family. Communication difficulties were not so drastic as he had been led to believe by other experts. The highest number of difficulties in this area occurred with boys (24 per cent of families), but in all except 4 per cent of those cases, the boys had been difficult to get through to prior to puberty as well. The study concedes that alienation may grow a little more acute in teenagers older than his study group, and in those old enough to work but still – through unemployment or higher education – dependent on parents.

What Rutter describes as 'inner turmoil', however, he found to be no myth. A fifth of the boys and girls reported being intermittently so depressed that they had trouble sleeping. Most of this misery was unnoticed by the adults in their lives.

The influence of friends becomes very strong by the age of 14/15, Rutter agreed. Strong enough to rival parental influence, but only in a minority of cases to replace it. Where serious trauma or psychiatric problems occurred in adolescence, they were rarely bolts from the blue. The signs of turmoil had been present in childhood too.

Parents waiting for some sort of adolescent timebomb to hit their family can take some comfort from the study. However, the fact remains that the overwhelming majority of parents I met had problems with their teenagers, and the teenagers had criticism of parents. Some problems, as with drugs and alcoholism were heartbreaking and home-wrecking.

Others were, to an outsider, merely the everyday hassles of two-generation family life. Maybe, as Michael Rutter and his colleagues suggest, the problems between most parents and teenagers are not life-and-death matters and relatively short-lived. But the proximity of family living and the intensity of the relationships blow them up out of proportion. And there can be long-term effects. Darwin Shreve, Head of an Assessment Centre for problem teenagers:

'People sometimes suggest it's a waste of money, time and energy sorting out teenagers' problems, when, in theory, the majority of them will grow out of them at around 20 years of age. Well, not all of them will, but even if they do, there will be scars left.

'They will have missed out on education – family problems and school difficulties go together – and there is a cycle of emotional damage. Young people whose own problems remain unresolved often make early, unwise marriages and have children they are not equipped to cope with. Those children run a high risk of developing problems themselves. I know; I'm old enough to be seeing a second generation of problem children on my own patch.'

The most oft-repeated sentence I heard in interviews was, 'They won't talk to us.' It came from both sides of the generation gap. The second most common utterance was a question, or a series of them, from parents: 'What do other families say? Do they have problems? How do they cope?'

Why hadn't they asked other families themselves? 'Because there is a stigma attached to being unable to handle your teenager,' explained Bill O'Connell, at the time head of a branch of Family Network, the counselling service for parents under stress. 'It's okay to admit to having trouble with your 4-year-old, but there's a feeling that by the time you are in middle-age and you've had all that practice, you should have got it right. To admit to a problem teenager makes you feel a failure, so people tend not to talk about it, and don't find out that the family next door is having exactly the same difficulties.'

2

What the helpers hear

Family Network sometimes runs self-help groups for parents of teenagers with specific problems. The one on young people who steal, for instance, was very well-attended, a clue to the size of that particular worry.

One of the off-shoots of 'keeping mum' about your kids is that you never find out what is normal behaviour and what other teenagers are up to. Teenagers are not above using the bit of blackmail which begins, 'But *everybody* does it. . . .' Such anxious parents frequently ring Family Network (This, and all organisations mentioned in the course of this book, are listed on pp. 178–180) to ask, 'Is this what other kids are doing nowadays? Is this normal? Am I being Victorian?' Bill O'Connell points out: 'There is no "normal". Every case depends on the relationship and whether the child is being treated appropriately for his age.

'Parents vary enormously in what they will accept. Some see no dangers in letting a 13-year-old attend all-night parties. Others won't let a 15-year-old out of the house past 9 o'clock. In general I'd say too many parents give in to their adolescents for a quiet life or because they are afraid of losing them. This is upsetting for a teenager. They find that if they lean against a wall, the wall falls down. Nothing in their world seems solid. You can end up with a spoiled 16-year-old, a larger version of a spoiled 3-year-old.'

'I'm talking about the boy who may throw temper tantrums, kick the furniture, deliver verbal and sometimes physical abuse when he doesn't get his own way. With a girl the problem is more likely to be that she is staying out late, keeping worrying company or Mum discovers she is on the pill or has had an abortion.

'You've got to give kids a framework, explain that you live by certain values and you want them to give it a try. They may rebel against those values, but at least they'll know where they stand. There have to be house rules.

'Some mothers over-mother their teenagers to the extent that they begin to think life is a four-star hotel. They should be prepared for independence; left to cook their own dinner if they insist on coming in late for meals, expected to tidy their bedrooms.

'On the other hand, parents shouldn't have such stern rules that kids feel freaks among their friends. They have to be flexible. Most of all they have to learn to hold a discussion with their son or daughter without attacking them.'

By the time Darwin Shreve sees adolescents at his Assessment Centre, family problems have become acute.

'The most common problem we see is the youngster of 14/15/16 beginning to spread his wings and demanding freedom to run his own life. The parents can't cope, the arguments build up to fever pitch, eventually the young person walks out or is chucked out and comes to the attention of first the Social Services Department and then us.

'Basically what goes wrong with parent-adolescent relationships, is that parents continue to treat their children as they did when they were 5 or 10-years-old. The teenager is making the transition to adulthood, but the parents have not made the transition to their child's adulthood and continue to lay down the law. The teenager reacts with rebellion and the result is stalemate. If somebody neutral steps in between the two warring factions to explain the facts of life – that the young person is not a child, but that parents have a responsibility for them and their behaviour – you may get somewhere.

'The most common cry you hear from social workers in this field is that a teenager is "out of control". The child comes here and we find that this is far from true. It is a problem of handling, and it is predominantly the fault of the parents. You only have to watch parents with their teenagers to see why. They still talk to them as if they are addressing a 7-year-old; they talk around them and about them. They never ask them to do something, they tell them. When their son or daughter is talking to them, they are walking around, looking at the ceiling, doing something else – indicating quite clearly that they are not listening, not really interested. They would never do that with another adult unless they were deliberately trying to antagonise them.

'In most cases the parents *are* listening to what is being said, but they have forgotten how to communicate this to their children. They have developed this particular style of half-communicating with their own children. Young children accept it, but adolescents won't. When teenagers say: "My parents don't listen to me" – as teenagers often do – they mean it.'

'I believe that as a good parent, you have to know when to act blind, deaf and dumb, and learn to take risks. If your 15-year-old daughter is brought home by her boy-friend and you accidentally-on-purpose happen to see they are having a prolonged necking session on the doorstep, what do you do? In my view, you do not rush out, drag her in and threaten him. You take the risk that they will know when to stop. If you want to talk about it, you pick another time.

'The way to understand a teenager is to look back at your own adolescent years. Circumstances change, but basic human feelings do not. All teenagers break the law, if only in minor ways. Many are attracted to a wild bunch, and flirt with their ideas, though they may have too much common-sense to step across the line and join them. They all tell lies. They have all done things they would not like their parents to know about, particularly in the area of sexuality. This applies as much to my generation as to the kids today. If we could get rid of the idea that our teenagers are a different species, we could use our own experience to understand them.'

Cynthia Leonard, Director of a branch of the Samaritans, never sees the teenagers who phone her organisation; she only hears the cries for help. She works in a small and rather affluent town, where young callers' problems vary from 'concern over spots and shyness to distress and insecurity at parents splitting up'.

'Parents have such high expectations. The more educated the parents, the higher the expectations. When young people cannot live up to this, the stress is enormous.

'Kids also feel acutely the unfairness of adults. They are told not to drink but Dad stays out all evening in the pub. Where teenagers are concerned, parents are very moralistic about sex, but then the young person finds out that Mum or Dad is having an affair. Parents seem to have one set of rules for their children and another for themselves.

'Add to this the usual adolescent worries – very real to them – about shyness, not getting on with people, failure with the opposite sex, and you see why some young people feel desperate. Parents often seem too busy to be bothered with their worries, and you can imagine what courage it takes to ring us and trust us not to give them away. If only parents would put themselves in their teenager's shoes sometimes.'

So is adolescence as a problem condition really necessary? Is it something that comes from within, triggered off by the physical and hormonal changes, or has society (i.e. you, me and the folks next door) created young people's problems by the way we treat them and organise their lives?

Frank Musgrove, in his book *Youth and the Social Order*, argues for the latter view. 'The adolescent as a distinct species is the creation of modern social attitudes and institutions,' he says. He deplores the 'age-segregated institutions' into which we place young people, including the colleges, youth clubs and apprenticeship schemes, and suggests that some 12 and 13-year-olds might be better spending time in part-time work, rather that in a school they dislike.

Adults, insists Frank Musgrove, segregate young people in a different world in order to protect their own power and authority. 'After 14 or 15, age needs to become an irrelevance in judging an individual's worth.'

Musgrove's theory is only one end of a wide spectrum. The middle and probably the majority view is that adolescent problems stem from a combination of internal (biological) factors and external (socio-cultural) factors.

3

Kids today: Life on their side of the gap

'Sad and terrible happenings had never made Frankie
cry, but this season many things made Frankie suddenly
wish to cry . . . things she had never noticed before
began to hurt her; home lights watched from the evening
sidewalks, an unknown voice from an alley . . . she was
afraid of these things that made her suddenly wonder
who she was, and what she was going to be in the world,
and why she was standing at that minute, seeing a light,
or listening, or staring up into the sky; alone.'

Carson McCullers *The Member of The Wedding*

Poor Frankie, 12⅚ years old, 5'5¾" tall, estimating that with her
growth rate, she will be over 9' tall by her 18th birthday! Another
time, another place, but she still typifies the self-consciousness and
the search for self so common to early adolescence.

When I was a teenager, reading magazine articles on how to make
the best of myself, and quizzes to find out what sort of person I was,
the bit of advice that foxed me was, 'Be yourself'.

I'd have been happy to oblige – if only I knew who or what this
all-important self was. You don't know who you are or where you
are going or what you'll be thinking in a year's time. It's exciting, it's
confusing. The whole of life is just around the corner.

Hence the trying out of different, and often bizarre clothes,
hairstyles, poses, interests, attitudes, friends and patterns of behaviour. Teenagers are trying on identities for size. By the end of
adolescence they'll have more or less settled for one, unless some
major emotional upheaval intervenes and prevents them from
maturing.

It may not be the identity parents would prefer, but it will be a
unique self, a whole individual, separate from their parents. That is
what adolescence is all about after all – separation.

Adolescence is also about letting go – the parents letting go of the
child in whom they have invested so much of their lives; the child
letting go of parents, of childhood, of safety. Letting go is never
easy, from either side of the generation gap.

It might be a lot easier if it was a simple, clean break, but adolescence is a long-drawn-out process that can stretch from around 11 years of age to around 20. It starts with the child/ adolescent stage, when, typically, the boy or girl is shy, self-conscious and very concerned with personal appearance. It's the stage when they spend hours staring into a mirror agonising over an invisible (to other people) spot.

At this stage the battles are likely to be about minor things like clothes and hairstyles – and the fact that parents insist on treating them like children. The middle period of adolescence – usually around 14, 15, 16, though times vary with individual maturity – is the traditional black spot. This is the stage at which they may question their parents' values and way of life and rebel against both.

They are egocentric and self-involved and see everything in black and white. They are constantly looking inside themselves – an exhausting business so they are liable to be somewhat lethargic! – and frequently 'want to be alone'. Parents often feel totally cut out of their children's lives – or are so irritated by the moodiness and rebellion that they choose to opt out! Almost certainly teenagers at this age see themselves as adults and demand the freedom to do their own thing without interference by parents. Parents usually see it differently, so it is the stage of daily battles.

Somewhere during the third stage of adolescence, teenagers become more aware of other people and their feelings. They are ready to come back to accepting their parents into their lives, not this time on a parent/child basis, but as equals. To reach this happy stage however, they have to progress through the other stages. If they are curtailed (by, for instance, early marriage or parenthood) they are more likely to be emotionally immature.

THE TASKS OF ADOLESCENCE. A NEW BODY.
This process of identity formation is one of the 'tasks' of adolescence that have to be completed. There are others. One of the earliest tasks is coming to terms with a new, sexually-mature body, at puberty. The whole process of puberty is spread over about five years. It can start as early as 8-years-old in girls (with the rudiments of breast development) and as early as 9 in boys.

That said, there is a wide range of 'normal'. Late-developing girls may be just embarking on the process as they approach 13, by which time their early-maturing friends will have passed right through to physical adulthood. Boys tend to be about a year behind girls, and today's teenagers perhaps a year ahead of their parents' generation.

Parents often don't realise their children have entered puberty, particularly with boys. The mother of a 13-year-old recalled her shock when visiting him in hospital. 'They told me he was in the bathroom. I knocked then pushed the door open – he always keeps it locked at home – and caught a glimpse of what I took to be a man getting out of the bath. I backed out hurriedly thinking I'd gone to the wrong room, but it was my son. I couldn't believe it, I thought he was still a little boy.'

Because of the teenage obsession with being in tune with their friends, both early and late developers have a difficult time. So do their parents. 'It can be very worrying having a 10½-year-old daughter who is shaped like Dolly Parton and has started her periods,' explained one mother. 'You are aware that boys are not to know by looking that she's still at Junior School. She'd be such easy prey, being innocent. You do not want to make her neurotic with too many warnings. It was terrifying to think about the situation she might find herself in and not know how to handle. But you can't lock them up, can you?'

In fact, more than 10 per cent of girls now have their first period whilst still at Primary School, and few schools are geared to cope with it. Boys maturing early are not so badly off, it merely puts them in step with most girls of the same age, and often gives them an advantage in sports and athletics. It can be a boost to self-confidence.

But for both sexes, there's a lot of pressure in having to behave as grown-up as you look, when you may still feel like a child inside. And there's the risk of teasing run by anyone who is a bit different.

Even more at risk of teasing are the late developers. Hardly a week passes without a letter in the teenage magazines Agony Columns which begins something like: 'I'm 13, and the only girl in my class who doesn't need a bra. I feel everyone is staring at me in the changing-room and thinking I'm abnormal. . . .'

Boys have no Agony Aunts to consult, but no-one who knows teenagers doubts that they can suffer unspoken agonies over being less well-developed than their peers. Long-term research shows that boys who mature late tend to be more tense, talkative, self-conscious and attention-seeking than their typically self-assured, early maturing friends.

NEW RELATIONSHIPS

'Just as a small child has to learn to stand, adolescence is a time of learning to stand on our own feet. A baby holds on to the furniture as it struggles to get its balance, an adolescent holds on to his or her own age group, in an emotional sense.'

Dr Edna Irwin, Psychiatrist

Friends are vitally important people in a teenager's life. More important than parents at a certain stage, some expert teen-watchers say. Having good ones can be the greatest source of happiness; being without them the biggest cause of distress. One 16-year-old girl who never thinks of worrying about the bomb or unemployment, admitted: 'My nightmare is to wake up one morning and find I haven't any friends. Imagine – having no-one to talk to and spend evenings with and having to stay in with the family!'

Friends are often a great source of worry to parents, blamed for much of what goes wrong in the family–child relationship. But the fact is that these friends – from the general 'crowd' to the 'best' friend are serving a useful purpose in a young person's develop-ment. On the experience of these friendships and what he learns from them, will be based his long-term adult relationships, and their success or failure.

Friends give support when an adolescent needs to (has to, if he's to achieve maturity) loosen the ties with parents. They are someone to share your problems – a sort of personal self-help group – when you can't talk openly to parents, because parents are part of those problems.

Belonging to the right group of friends means dressing in a certain way, following a particular style of music (always loud), frequenting the right club, affecting the right language. The details and the rapidity with which they change are mind-boggling to adults. The first time your first teenager demands a hideously ugly coat (to adult eyes) or comes home with green hair can be a terrible shock.

With subsequent styles the shock lessens. Parents adapt . . . most of them anyway. It becomes a question not of 'Under no circum-stances will a child of mine colour his/her hair,' but 'Wouldn't that delicate burgundy suit you better than the green streaks?' It is, in the long run, a relatively harmless, temporary way of satisfying a need for independence.

Belonging, fitting in, is desperately important. Carson McCullers in *The Member of the Wedding* tells us of the yearning, sad Frankie, 'It was the Summer when for a long time she had not been a member. She belonged to no club and was a member of nothing in the world. Frankie had become an unjoined person who hung around in doorways and she was afraid.'

As they get to the mid-teens, adolescent friendships become more intimate – and consequently, more liable to painful disrup-tion. It is the age of the best friend, which gradually eases the way into heterosexual relationships. Friendships among girls are likely to be deep and more emotionally-dependent. Boys' friendships are more outwardly competitive – they opt for a 'good mate' rather than a same-sex companion to share their deepest anxieties.

RELATIONSHIPS WITH THE OPPOSITE SEX

All the teenagers and all the parents I spoke to had views on this subject, and it is dealt with later in the book. Suffice to say that such relationships are a major part of growing up – probably the most publicised part.

NEW MIND/NEW DIRECTIONS

From around the age of 12, young people move from thinking only in simple practical terms to being able to think in the abstract. It means they can examine their own thoughts and feelings; can analyse, predict and conclude. It also means that they can – and do – take issue with their parents' beliefs and their way of life and scorn and criticise them. Enter the teenage rebel!

Suddenly they can see everything that is wrong with the world. What's more they – and only they – have the formula for putting it right. This usually involves anarchy and total re-organisation of the Establishment. Certainly it involves hours of argument. It's more likely to be talk than action. Parents are torn between irritation at the know-all arrogance and pride – even inferiority – at their child's display of deep thinking.

NEW MORALS

It can be very painful for parents to have everything they hold dear scorned by their son or daughter. It creates a further complication for the teenager too. If he is no longer able to accept his parents' social, political and religious (to name but a few) beliefs, then he has to formulate his own moral code of conduct.

Whose guidelines should he use? Parents (he is still absorbing some of their values whilst rebelling against them) say one thing, friends say another. Friends may be divided into several factions. Forces as far afield as the media and the church are fighting for his mind, and maybe his soul.

'At no time in life is a person as likely to be concerned with moral values – with what is right and true, wrong or false – as during adolescence,' writes John Conger in *Adolescence – Generation under Pressure*. Choosing is not easy.

To these traditional tasks of growing up, add the newer ones we inflict on adolescents – doing well in exams, getting (against almost impossible odds) a job, fitting into the new, extended families constructed from divorce and re-marriage – and you can see that adolescence is not the carefree time we adults tend to remember it as.

It *can* be joyous, of course. So many experiences are fresh and new and there's the promise of excitement around every corner. The highs will never be so high again, but neither will the lows be so low. As Theodore Roethke in *Collected Verse – I'm Here*, reminds us 'So much of adolescence is an ill-defined dying, an intolerable waiting, a longing for another place or time, another condition.'

4

Teenagers talking . . .

Sally:
'I can get round my Dad, but never my Mum. If he's mad about something you just keep talking to him, even if he ignores you. Or you give him something to eat. Food always puts him in a good mood.

'My Mum is really strict though. I've got two older sisters but that hasn't made her more easy-going. It's made her worse, because one of my sisters was attacked near the school and she's worried that it will happen to me.

'You know how you see some mothers and daughters out shopping or walking along the street and they are linking arms? You couldn't ever do that with my Mum. She doesn't want you to get near her. With talking too, you keep your distance. You can't talk to her about personal things. You wouldn't want to. You know she wouldn't like it. I can tell her I'm going out with a boy, but you can't tell her anything about feelings.

'She thinks girls my age are totally innocent. Well, we're not all *doing* anything with lads, but we all *know* what there is to know. We've known for years. My Mum seems to think she's kept it secret.

'The other day I said something to my sister about someone having a lovebite and Mum said "Where did you hear about things like that?" My Dad is different. He makes jokes about what you might be up to – though he wouldn't like it if he thought it was true. He sings about my boyfriends. He makes up little songs about them. Honestly! And if you're talking to a boy on the phone, he takes the receiver and shouts "She loves you." He sounds raving mad when you try to tell someone about him, doesn't he?

'I don't drink. It's a waste of money and it's horrible. I smoke though, about ten a day. My Mum and Dad would kill me if they found out, especially my Dad, so I can't smoke at home. I started because everyone else was doing it and now I can't give it up.

'My Mum gives me the money for it without knowing. I mean if I'm going out to a disco I'll tell her it costs more than it does, then use the spare cash for cigarettes.

'My Mum buys my clothes but only when I'm with her. She used to go out and come back with these awful shoes and expect me to wear them. I refused and we used to have awful rows. I mean you couldn't go outside and let your mates see you in some of the things parents expect you to wear. She used to really yell at me and threaten not to buy me any more but still I wouldn't wear them. I'd bash them on the school walls to make them look worn down or pull the heel off and say it had fallen off. She usually fell for that. There was this unbelievable sheepskin coat of my sister's she tried to make me wear. I took it to school and "lost" it.

'They just don't understand the way you dress. She thinks if she's seen a picture of it in a magazine or the girl down the road wearing something I'll wear it. But you wear your own style. People know what you are by what you wear. I'm into jazz funk. By the time my mother has caught on to that – if she ever does – I'll have moved on. Anyway, now she gives me the money or comes with me and I choose.'

Colin:
'The other thing about clothes is they always think they can get them cheaper. You say, "I need £20 for a pair of trainers" and they say "What? I can get you a pair down the road for £4". The ones they've seen are nothing like the ones you want, and everyone but your parents would know it. Styles change fast. It's no good your Mum saying when you ask for a pair of shoes "What's wrong with the pair you've got on? I only got you those a few months ago." I mean if there's something new out, you look out of place in the old ones. I dress pretty straight. I like this pale grey leather jacket. I like to look fairly smart. My Mum and my step-father pay for clothes. I mean it's your parents' responsibility to buy your clothes, isn't it? But if I get some cash for Christmas or a birthday I often spend it on clothes.

'My Mum gives me £5 on a Thursday, her pay-day, but that doesn't go very far. A couple of times in the week I'll ask her if I can have a pound and she can take it out of my next pocket money. She gives it me, then forgets to dock it. She knows I smoke and she doesn't mind, as long as I don't smoke upstairs. Cigarettes cost you more in the holidays because you have to buy your own all the time. At school you can bag seconds or thirds off someone who's got some, at break-times. One ciggie is passed down the line. Mind you it's not much fun being the one who gets the last puff. I've got quite a bad chest. I get smoker's cough in the morning.

'I drink. Everyone does. But I'm not roaring drunk every night or anything. My Mum doesn't mind me coming home after a few too many beers if I go straight to bed and don't bother her. She gets mad though if I feel like starting an argument or playing the fool.'

Andy:

'My dad doesn't live with us, and my mother has mostly stopped telling me what to do now. Apart from one thing – she doesn't allow smoking in the house. Maybe it's a good job I don't smoke.

'Drinking's okay. I suppose most of my money goes on drink. I can get served in a pub with no bother. It's where me and my mates spend most of our time, especially at weekends. It's a laugh and it's the only place to go if you don't fancy dancing.

'I certainly don't spend my money on clothes. An old T-shirt and jeans are what I usually wear, plus a black leather jacket. Outside school, my mates are hippies. We wear our hair long usually. I've just had mine cut to stop my Mum nagging for a bit. She's always on when she sees one of the lads from school like Colin. It's "Why can't you look respectable like him?"

'No disrespect, but I don't look like him because I'd feel a right fool dressed up "fashionable". It's not me. That's not the group I feel at home with. I've never tried to explain it to her. You try to tell her anything and it's, "Don't talk to me, I know."

'My mother's okay, but she's like all parents. They know it all. They never want to listen to your side of the story. That's the thing that really makes me mad about older people. It makes me feel like going out and smashing up a few phone boxes when they treat me like that. But they're all smashed already around here!

'There's just one other thing my mother does that drives me mad. She calls me "bab" in front of my mates. At sixteen, I ask you! I wish she wouldn't.'

Maureen:

'I get on with my Mum. We agree about most things. My Dad *never* agrees with me, particularly about me going out. I just take no notice of him, except to tell him where I'm going and what time I'll be back. If I go to a disco or something I can stay out till 10.30; if it's just going down my friend's house, I have to come back for 9.30. If I'm late, he moans at my Mum. Sometimes he sends her out to search for me, so it's a bit unfair to her. Trouble is he's out of work, so he's at home all day, watching my every move.'

Carole:

'It's just the same in our house. I can talk to Mum about anything but Dad is really old-fashioned. He thinks we should be brought up as strictly as he was. His rules are funny really. I can't smoke but he doesn't mind me having a drink. I can go to a club and stay till 2 in the morning, as long as he knows where I am, when I'll be home and who I'm with. And as long as I'm not with a boy. That's the one big rule.

'Boys are his big worry. I'm not officially allowed to go out with them at all. If one calls for me, he gets really annoyed. He won't talk about it. You can't get him to say when, if ever, he thinks I'll be old enough. It's just "Shut up, do as I say."

'My older sister was different from me, more rebellious, and he was even stricter with her. She wouldn't put up with it. She left home at 18. Then she got pregnant. She's married to her boy-friend now and has a baby. She's cut herself off from home. We haven't seen her in over a year, because of my Dad's attitude. He never talks about her, but I know Mum misses her and is worried that I'll do the same.

'I won't though. I can put up with him, as long as Mum takes my part. I don't mean she stands up to him – she doesn't. But I do go out with boys and she knows, we keep it from Dad. I'll say I'm going out with one of my girl-friends and Mum will cover for me. What he doesn't know won't hurt him, she says.'

Trisha:
'My Dad is completely different, you can tell him anything. It was my mother who was strict. Dad is the softie. She left when I was 12. She lives with her boy-friend. My young brother goes to see her every weekend, but my sister and I don't. I don't regard her as my mother now. I say hello if I see her in the street. For the first couple of years I wouldn't even speak to her. She wrote us a few letters telling us how much she missed us and that. Hard luck – it was her who left.

'I don't really miss having a mother; only when there's a lot of housework to do. But we've got a routine now – my sister and I do it between us. It's quite nice, really, running the house. I don't expect there's anything Carole would tell her mother that I couldn't tell my father. I haven't got a boy-friend, but he's talked to me about it. He says if I want to sleep with a boy, it's okay by him if I go on the pill. He'd just like me to be sensible. If I want to smoke he won't mind. What he doesn't want is for me to do things behind his back. He just wants us all to be honest with him.'

Maureen:
'I wouldn't tell my mother anything like that. She wouldn't like it and there's no point in upsetting her. As for my Dad, I never have a conversation long enough to find out what he feels about anything. I don't think I'd fancy living with a boy myself. I'd like to get married at about 19 and have a couple of kids straight away, while I'm young

enough to enjoy them. I'd like to join the police force too, but I don't know if I have much chance of getting in. There's more chance of getting married!'

Trisha:
'I want to get married, but not yet. Carole and I are going to try to get into college and train as nursery nurses. I'd like to have a bit of a career first. I'd hate to think I'd never have a job and would have to hang around on the dole till I got married.'

Carole:
'I'll probably leave home when I'm about 18. I might get a job as a nanny. It's the only way I'll ever have a chance to find someone to marry, with my Dad around.'

Martin: who lives with his widowed mother and 18-year-old brother:
'I can't remember my father's face or anything he ever did for me, though he's only been dead a few years. I think that's very sad. I wouldn't tell my mother, because it would hurt her. When the family talk about him, I pretend to remember. I miss him – or rather, I miss having somebody around who might understand me.

'My mother certainly doesn't, and I can't stand my brother. All my life it's been thrown in my face that James is the one with the brains and poor old Martin is thick. Oh, they don't say it, but it's obvious.

'He's the one who's at college. I'll have to leave school at 16 and grovel around looking for any job that brings in a wage to help support the family. Yet he's the blue-eyed boy. When I say this to my mother, she says it isn't true and has hysterics. She has hysterics a lot, my mother. Maybe she has trouble taking on two roles, mother and father.

'I don't have any relationship with either my mother or my brother. I speak to them but I don't talk to them; I spend most of the time in my room alone. If I casually mention something about jobs to my mother, she gets very serious and starts talking about what I should do with my life. It gets on my nerves. We never seem able to communicate at the same level, so it's best to keep to myself.

'My brother's had a few tries at being "the man of the house" and telling me what to do. I soon put paid to that. I'm bigger than him now. I'm not lonely, not really. I have my mates, and I'm a bit of a day-dreamer anyway.

'My biggest problem is this girl, Sue, that I've been crazy about for ages. Four years actually. I don't know why I feel like this about her. She's not the best-looking girl in the world. The girl I'm going out with – and trying to get rid of – is better-looking. But I can't get Sue out of my mind. I see her every day – she lives in my road – and I think about her day and night.

'I expect she hates me, I've pestered her so much. Her mother knows – probably from all the time I've spent kissing the doorstep! Everyone at school knows. I've asked her over and over to tell me why she won't go out with me, and she just says she doesn't want to. I'd feel better about it if she had a boy-friend. At least there would be a reason I could understand.

'I go out with other girls, but only if they make the running, and I get fed up with them quickly. Like this girl at the moment. She's nice, but she bores me. What's the point of going out with a girl when you feel nothing for her? Some lads do it just to prove they can pull birds or they're not queer.

'I really get cheesed off with life. What is there to look forward to, with the job situation, and Sue? I think I'll give it two or three years to see how things work out, and then I'm going to try to be a priest. My mates think it's a laugh, but I'm serious. I think I'd be a good priest.'

Adrian, the youngest of 9 children:
'Most of my brothers and sisters have left home. I wish my older brother would leave. He makes my life a misery. He gets me up at 7 every morning to fetch the papers for him, even during school holidays. Mum just says, "Well he pays you for doing it."

'I don't want paying; I just don't want to do it. Brothers can be worse than parents for bossing you about. The only advantage in having a big family is they are always giving you money. My parents are okay. They're out of touch, of course. I don't talk to my Dad much, but I listen a lot. He talks about what life was like 40 years ago and how much you could buy for one-and-sixpence. He's old, over 60 probably. I've never asked.

'I'm not sure he remembers half the time which of us is which. I'm closer to my Mum. The youngest always is, I think, though a boy never gets really close. Not like some of the girls you see out with their Mums shopping and giggling as if they were best mates. It must be nice to get on like that with your Mum or Dad, but boys never do.'

OUT OF SCHOOL AND 'ON A SCHEME'

Peter, 16 years old, a rebel with or without a cause, in an Action-Man combat jacket:

'I'm on a Youth Training Scheme as a mechanic, but there's very little chance of a job at the end of it. It doesn't worry me; I don't lose any sleep. There's work around if you want it badly enough. I could pick up a few pounds doing casual work round where I live, repairing people's cars.

'All this talk about the need to work. I don't have any need to work, except to pay the bills and to get enough money for a motor-bike. That's all I want; a bike of my own. Then I can get on it and take off, get as far away as I want to. Where would I go? Oh, I don't know. It's riding the bike and the freedom to go that's important.

'I've wanted a bike since I was 11 and me and a mate took one off the street and went ride-about. We were stopped by the police and I was taken home by the strong arm of the law. My old man wasn't exactly delighted. He knocked me around like the ball on a pin-ball machine. He doesn't do much of that now, but then he's a sick man – I mean really ill, though he still manages to go to work.

'I don't live at home much, not if I can help it. I stay there occasionally. I get on with them if I keep my distance, but they think I don't care about anyone except myself. I expect they're right. All I really ask is to be allowed to lead my own life, without being supervised by the older generation or the police or someone. I've been in trouble with the police off and on. Just little things; I'm not a hardened criminal. It might be that some kids had been doing a bit of nicking and I'm receiving. But once that happens, they've always got their eye on you. They won't leave you alone. Anything goes missing, they're round your house straight away.

'When you get to 16 or so, you want to be free to go out with your mates without somebody telling you to get home early because you have to get up for school or work in the morning. You don't want to have to say where you are going and when you'll be home. For a while the old man tried to treat me the way he'd treat my older sister – expecting me to be in before midnight like I was Cinderella or something. That's okay for girls, but it's different for a lad. You can handle yourself. Nobody's going to rape you.

'I stood up to him, told him I wasn't going to go along with his rules, to put it politely. And he just gave in. I couldn't believe it – I thought he was nuts to tell you the truth. I was disappointed. I like a good argument. I wanted to fight it out and be the winner. One half of me wanted him to be my father and tell me what to do – even though I had no intention of doing it.

'He's a funny bloke my old man. He'd hit me himself, but if he ever saw anyone else pick on me, an older bloke, he'd be knocking hell out of him in seconds. It toughens you up being brought up that way. You're no cissy. But it also makes you hard, especially with girls. If you're with a girl and there's a row and she starts crying, you don't feel sympathy. You just say, "Oh, shut up for God's sake."

'Mostly I get on okay with girls though. You treat them as you find them. If a girl is a bit of a slag, you go for the whole business straight away. If she's a good girl, you treat her with respect. The only time my parents have talked to me about sex was once when they came home and found me upstairs with a girl.

'My old man called me down. I thought he might kill me but he was very good. He told me to take the girl home and then had a little talk about the dangers of getting a girl into trouble. The funny thing was, on that particular occasion, what me and the girl were doing upstairs was looking for a record I was going to lend her!

'I feel my parents have got a bit of a grudge against me. I don't think I turned out the way they'd have picked; not like my sister who's very clever and did well at school. I hated school. It bored me out of my mind. The only parts I liked were woodwork and metalwork and motor vehicle lessons. I'm good with my hands, but parents don't appreciate that. They like you to be good at passing O-levels.

'Sometimes I get really fed up. You think things are going well, then it collapses. You're getting on with your parents then they turn against you; you're going out with a girl and it's great, then suddenly it's boring and it's nothing. I can't explain but it happens to me all the time. Everything I touch turns to shit.'

Patrick, 17 years old, soberly dressed and thoughtful. He is half-way through a YTS office training scheme, hopes to get a job somewhere else if not here at the end of it:

'My problem is my older brother. He's super-intelligent – he's got 13 O-levels, and 4 Grade-A A-levels. He's waiting to take the Oxbridge exam and filling in with a job in California. He got this amazing job with no trouble, while I had to take a £25 a week YTS scheme. My younger brother looks like being the same, so you can imagine how I feel; the dum-dum in the middle. Really peed off.

'My parents don't rub it in, but they don't have to. They are both teachers and they know our capabilities to the last IQ point. My two brothers were sent to public school. They knew I wouldn't pass the entrance exam so I didn't take it. I had to make do with the local grammar school. Okay, it's a good school; there's great competition for places when you're 11, but it's a long way behind the one my brother went to.

'To make it worse, the one thing I'm better than both my brothers at, sport, I suddenly lost interest in. It got to be too much like hard work. That upset Dad. He's a health fanatic, out running all the time, though he's 50 now. He hates smoking, so I'd never smoke in the house. I'm still fairly fit and keen on sport, but I haven't lived up to my potential in that area either. I want my parents to think well of me. I'd like to live up to their ideals, but I can't.

'Maybe they're not so disappointed; maybe some of it is in my own mind. I get on okay with them now, though there was a bad patch at around fourteen or fifteen. Then they disapproved of everything I did and I thought they were the worst people in the world. They look more like human beings now. There was a really great moment this year, when my Dad put his arm round my shoulder and said "Want to come down to the pub for a drink?" An equal at last!

'My Mum is very naive. I think most parents are. She'll say things like, "Have you ever been to a party where there were drugs?" I mean what do you say? Have I ever been to a party where there *weren't* drugs of some kind? They are there if you want them. I don't. I don't need them. I've tried pot but it didn't do much apart from make me dizzy.

'I talk to my parents, but don't tell them the gory details. I don't think they want to know. My mother found a packet of Durex in my pocket when she was washing some clothes. She just laughed and handed them back to me. It was less embarrassing than I'd have thought, really. I suppose in this last year or so they've just accepted I'm an adult.

'I think your family go on being important to you, though some lads won't admit it. If somebody picked on my little brother, I'd really go for him. Or my big brother, come to that! But your mates are very important too. It's a bit rough when one of them starts going out with a girl and deffs you out. You know he's acting like a bit of a wally, but you know it could have been you and not him. However hard you try not to, you change when you are seriously involved with a girl.

'I think boys are more loyal to their mates than girls though. If you break up with a girl, they'll accept you back in the crowd. A girl who has given up her mates for a boy doesn't seem to get them back.

'The thing to remember when you start going with a girl is that it isn't going to last forever, not at your age. The first time a girl ditches you, it's very painful, but you get hardened to it after a few times!

'You'd be out of your mind to think of getting married in your teens. It's okay to live with a girl. It's okay to have a busy sex life – if you can get it! Well, it's okay for a boy, not for a girl. If I take a girl out and she sleeps with me straight away, I may enjoy it, I may have gone out of my way to persuade her, but I'm still not going to think a lot of her. I'm sorry, I didn't make the rules, but that's how it is.'

GIRL TALK – 16/17 YEAR OLDS

Geraldine, 17 years old, on a Youth Training Scheme in the office of a large factory. Her parents were both married before. She has sisters, a brother and half-brothers:
'I'm my father's only daughter and he's always been very over-protective about me. He used to be awful. A couple of years ago, I had to be in by 9 p.m., but at the same age my brother could wander in around 10.30 p.m. or later and nobody would say a word.

'It got so bad at one stage that I stayed out all night as a sort of protest. What happened was that he found me chatting to a group of boys, on the corner of our road in broad daylight, and he ordered me inside as if I was a 5-year-old. My friend's father had actually locked her in her room for an evening around the same time, so we decided to make a protest.

'We wandered round the streets till seven next morning. We were terrified of going home. They were all gathered in my friend's house. They'd rung the police and everything. It was my Mum who shouted at me. My Dad just went very quiet. I think he knew he had overdone the control bit. He's never been as bad since.

'I'm fond of him, but he doesn't really understand me. My Mum does. Sometimes I think she can read my mind. The day I started my periods, it was a bit of a shock. I went into the bathroom, discovered what had happened, and called down, "Mum". She arrived at the door in seconds with a sanitary towel in her hand!

'We've often sat up till the early hours of the morning talking. She knows I sleep with my boy-friend. It was my Mum who first suggested I go on the pill. I was 15 and going to a lot of parties. She didn't try to stop me, but she was frightened I'd get drunk and do something I mightn't have done sober.

'We went to the doctor's together. We pretended I wanted the pill for irregular periods – a lot of girls get it on those grounds – but he said he didn't approve of it unless it was absolutely necessary. I went to the clinic when I had a reason, a steady boy-friend, and there was no problem.

'I didn't tell my Dad but he found out – I think. I dropped my clinic card and he picked it up and handed it to me. "I think this is yours", was all he said, and I didn't dare say anything because I didn't know how much he had grasped.

'I've no idea what he thinks about anything, because we don't talk on that level. To him, I'm just his daughter, not an adult with opinions of her own. He wouldn't like some of my views. He's not stupid. He knows what goes on in the world. He knows what other girls do. But parents, fathers anyway, always have this hope that their daughter will be different. Sort of innocent forever.

'My mother is completely down-to-earth. Both my sisters were pregnant and married in their teens. She says she blames herself for not talking to them enough when they were my age. She's not going to make the same mistake with me.'

Josie, 17 years old, on an Office Skills course:
'If I had to go to one of my parents with a problem, I suppose I'd pick my Dad. But usually I go to my older sister. I can tell her anything and she doesn't look shocked and disappointed. My Mum is the last person you could tell. She's terribly straight-laced. She's never told me anything girls should know. When I started my periods I couldn't bring myself to tell her for ages. When I did, she just said, "Fine, okay". I suppose she figured I'd know enough having older sisters around.

'Being the youngest, most of the family have this image of me as the sweet little thing, the baby. I try to live up to it. I'd hate them to be disgusted with me, and they would be, if they knew I've been on the pill since I was 16. When my mother found out my sister was on the pill, she refused to speak to her for weeks . . . and she's 22. I wouldn't have dared take it under sixteen in case my parents were informed.

'My mother has never told me, in so many words what she disapproves of, but she makes it very clear. Once there was a programme on television about contraceptives and young girls, and she just turned and pointed her finger at me. "You wouldn't, would you?" was all she said. I shook my head and played little innocent again. I make myself sick sometimes. What I should have said was, "Would you prefer me to be pregnant?", but I don't have the nerve.'

Vicki, 17 years old, on a Youth Training Scheme. Her parents were divorced when she was 9, re-united two years later, then re-married: 'I hardly ever see my father. He's on night-work, so he's going out as I get in, or the other way round. Sometimes I feel I see too much of my mother! She tries to run my life, but I won't let her.

'Take my boy-friend; we've been going out together for four years. I've never been out with anyone else. We're getting engaged soon. But my Mum won't accept that I know my own mind. She's always telling me I should get to know other boys before I settle down.

'She thinks he doesn't treat me properly, because he goes out with his mates three times a week and I stay in on those days. I should be out with my own friends, she thinks – but I've sort of drifted out of the group now.

'Mum thinks I should be trying harder to get a job. Yet my sister is at home all the time, dossing about, never bothering to even get on a scheme, but my mother never nags her.

'She's always on at me to go out and enjoy myself. But the thing is, I only enjoy myself when I'm with my boy-friend. I know exactly what I want. I want to get married as soon as possible, and I want a baby. I wouldn't really mind if I got pregnant now, though I think my Dad would have something to say.

'My boy-friend and I started sleeping together about a year after we first went out. You don't plan these things. They just happen if you love each other. My mother was shattered – well, more hurt really, when I told her. I couldn't understand it. I thought she knew. Parents can see exactly what the neighbours are doing, but they can be very blind about their own kids.'

Elizabeth, 13 years old, an only child:
'My mother would hate me to be sexist or racist. (I'm not either, but I throw in the words for black or Asian people that they use at school sometimes, just to see the horrified look on her face.) The thing is though, she's age-ist. Most parents are. I mean they think you should have no rights and that your opinions aren't worth anything, because you're a different age to them.

'They tell you what you should wear, when you should go to bed, who you should be friendly with, even what to think, when you're perfectly capable of deciding for yourself from the time you're 11 or 12. Well, most kids are – a few of them will always do the stupid thing. Parents ought to know you well enough to know if you are sensible.

'Take school. School really depresses me. It tires me out. It's nearly 5 o'clock when I get home, and then there's homework and that hardly leaves any time for anything else. I don't think parents have any idea how exhausting school is. But even so, if, tomorrow, I was told I could choose whether I went or stayed at home, I'd probably still go. I know it's important to learn, and to pass exams, and get a job – and for that you have to go to school. Sometimes though I think dossing around on the dole sounds like more fun than working and worrying over 'A'-levels.

'My father is never satisfied. When I come top in a few subjects, he just asks why I didn't do the same in all the others. He doesn't trust me either. If I say I'm going to meet my friend, you can see his mind ticking over, wondering if I'm secretly off to meet a boy – shock, horror! Unless they're picking me up, I have to be in by 8 p.m., and if I'm five minutes late, he'll nag my Mum to ring my friend's house. He disapproves of everything about me really – he moans about my clothes, my hair, the way I talk, the music I like. It doesn't bother me much, only that he thinks he's got the right to force his taste on to me.

'I suppose I get on okay with my Mum, though she's a bit fussy over where I go and what time I have to be back. We're more alike and she's more in touch with pop music and what's fashionable. Not that we agree. I think she wears awful clothes, but at least she doesn't try to force me to wear the same. She laughs at the things I wear, which isn't very polite, but is better than my father taking it dead seriously and freaking. I suppose it's easier for a Mum – she can remember being a teenage girl.

'I think my mother has improved over the last couple of years. She was awful at first when I wanted to choose my own look, trying to make me wear little Marks and Spencer dresses and have my hair cut the way *she* wanted. We had a lot of rows, but she gradually came round. Now she tries to force me to be trendier!

'She said to me recently, "You were awful last year; you're a lot more reasonable now." But the thing is *she*'s the one who was awful last year. She's the one who's had to be more reasonable. I think she's growing up!'

Emma, 16 years old, about to take 9 O-levels, lives just outside an affluent town. Her parents are divorced:
'I don't worry about the bomb – if it drops, it drops – or the shortage of jobs. My nightmare is to wake up one morning and find I've got no friends and have to stay in every night.

'There's a whole crowd of us, boys and girls, who meet in a pub in the town. I love the atmosphere in pubs though I don't drink. Anyway, there's nowhere else. I've grown out of discos and my Mum won't let me go to night clubs yet.

'For a while I pretended to her that we used to go to MacDonalds. Imagine sitting there every night over a Big Mac! I let it out because I can't keep secrets. She doesn't mind really, as long as I'm in by 11 p.m.

'I can see why she won't let me go to clubs. They are in the nearest city, which is a bit rough. That doesn't mean I won't keep nagging to go, but at least I understand the rules. I used to see no point in the rules she made. I believed she stopped me doing things to spite me.

'A couple of years ago, Mum used to object to me going to a park over the road, because she didn't like the kids who hung around there. At the time I thought they were very tough and interesting. We reached a compromise. I went, but for a shorter time than I wanted. I got tired of them pretty soon. If she'd banned me altogether, I'd probably have got really involved with them.

'The boy I'm going out with was one of that crowd, but he's quietened down a lot. He used to throw me in the nettle patch. My mother hated him. Before she'd let me go out with him, she made him come and apologise to her. She doesn't mind us going out together, but she won't leave us alone in the house if she's out in the evening.

'That's one of her daftest rules. Whatever she's worried about – we don't need a house to do it. It's not nice to feel you're not trusted. You feel why should you bother to try and do the right thing.

'I've one friend who's totally immoral but most of my friends are quite moral. If you are easy, or just go out with a lot of boys in our school, you are looked down on. Maybe it's different in other areas. A lot of what you believe depends where you grow up and what your friends think. My crowd think drugs are disgusting. We don't meet anyone on them. Mind you, we think the same about smoking and my two best friends smoke! They can't give it up.

'My mother is strict in some ways, not in others. Different parents have different ideas on what's wrong, don't they? I have a friend whose parents will let her go to clubs and stay out as late as she fancies, but they won't allow her to stay in someone's house or have friends to stay. Exactly the opposite to my Mum.

'I used to think the perfect parents were those who let their daughters do just what they wanted, no questions asked. Now I think that's just not caring. I'd like my mother to be a bit less fussy (she still makes me eat every scrap of my dinner because I'm thin) and allow me to make my own decisions. It's no good imposing your ideas of right and wrong on someone at sixteen. If they haven't learned by then, it's too late.

'You also learn by this age, how to get round parents, how to say the right thing. It's difficult when your parents are divorced, because you have to learn two sets of rules, one for each. The advantage is that you get two sets of pocket money – which, in my case, goes on clothes.

'I get a separate dress allowance off Mum. I got that by telling her that *everyone* but me got an allowance, when maybe two or three people I knew did. Then most of my friends worked the same trick on their parents, by trotting me out as an example!

Belinda, 17 years old, one of twins:

'I feel really sorry for our Mum sometimes. We really pick on her. We gang up on her, me and my sister, and argue if she tries to make us do something like housework. If there's an argument, she's the one who ends up in tears, not us.

'They don't really force any rules on us now. We go where we want to and say what time we'll be back. If it's late, say we're at a night club which doesn't finish till well past midnight, we come home in a taxi. Our parents worry we'll get raped or mugged waiting for an all-night bus in town, so four or five of us club together and pay for a taxi home. It's quite cheap that way. I'd hate to have to rely on a boy taking me home!

'None of our crowd want to settle down yet, though some of us have boy-friends. I know girls who have been going out with the same boy for centuries and only have one ambition, to get married and live happily ever after. They are really boring. They have no friends because they don't put any effort into getting on with other people. In the end, they have no choice but to spend all their time with their equally-boring boy-friend, who's lost all his mates too and probably resents it.

'We don't tell our parents much about what we do. Nor what other people do – they'll only assume we do it too! My older brother is the nosiest. He's much bossier than either Mum or Dad. He's always asking questions and accusing us of things. It's none of his business. You need an adult to talk to though, preferably somebody who doesn't live in the same house.

'My sister and I always go to our aunt if we have a problem, or if we just want to talk to someone older. I don't know why she's so good. She's not all that young – older than Mum actually – but she's more realistic somehow. She knows what goes on out in the world. Mum expects us to be perfect, but our aunt just expects us to be ourselves.'

Ellen, 16 years old, at a large Comprehensive:

'I think a lot of the ideas parents have about teenagers they get from watching television, so they only hear about the problems. I mean some of us are fairly normal. We've got common-sense and we're not going to take up something stupid like glue-sniffing just because we hear that lots of other kids are doing it.

'I'm not prim. I like boys. If I wanted to sleep with one when I was a bit older and have a steady relationship I wouldn't see anything wrong with it (though my Dad might!) But some of the girls at my school really have packed a lot of living into 16 or 17 years!

'My Dad reckons some of them are burned-out wrecks at 16! I'd say about 45 per cent of the 14–18 year olds are on the pill. No, I'm not exaggerating. They can't wait to tell you. But I reckon the thing has almost gone round full-circle and morality is coming back. More girls are having the confidence to say no. I mean, if you've done all that at 16, what have you got left?

'I've been going out with boys since I was 14 (my sister's that age now and she's not a bit interested!) I had this one boy-friend for nearly two years. My parents kept saying I should be going out with lots of people and having a good time. I didn't really believe them. I thought they were just worried that the relationship was getting too heavy with us being together all the time.

'But eventually I began to feel I was missing out. All my friends were dressing up and going out and I was like an old married woman at 15, so I broke it off.

'I go to night clubs in town with about five of my friends. It's a long way, but out in the suburbs, there's nothing for teenagers. Dad will pick me up at around midnight, if I haven't got a boy-friend with a car bringing me home.

'I have lots of boy-friends now. Mum says you've got to get to know plenty of them so you'll know which one is Mr Right! She approves of what I do. Dad I'm not so sure about. He's very, very hard to understand. The truth is he's not happy about me having boy-friends, whether it's one for two years or a different one each week.

'Mum says he doesn't like to see anyone trying to take his little girl away. For a week or so when I start going out with a new boy, he's very weird. He is miserable and depressed and doesn't talk much. Then gradually, when he gets to know the boy, he brightens up and comes back to normal. He can be very scathing. In the early days he used to make my first boy-friends feel like little kids with his remarks.

'Even now, we have terrible rows over boys. Last night I asked him if my current boy-friend, who's in the army, could come away with us on holiday. He exploded. He thought it was a disgusting suggestion.

'He doesn't explain why. You can't get logical reasons out of him. Part of it is that he doesn't like the idea of any boy coming in and breaking up his family. He wants us to be a little unit forever.

'Mum reckons there should be courses for parents, particularly fathers of teenagers, like the courses for parents of babies and toddlers – so they will get to understand how young people grow up.

'Dad's quite easy-going in some ways. He likes to see me in make-up, with my hair done and wearing stiletto heels and fashionable clothes. He'll object if I'm *not* done up.

'Both my parents have always had confidence in me, and that's made me more sure of myself than a lot of girls my age. For instance, I don't worry about getting a job any more. I've recently been ringing people up trying to find a holiday job, and I've been offered a lot of full-time jobs instead. I'm sure it's having the confidence to approach employers that does the trick.

'Sometimes my parents have a bit too much confidence in me. They let me have a party for my 15th birthday, while they kept out of the way; A real grown-up affair with alcohol, and me in charge as the hostess. There weren't any real disasters, though we had gate-crashers. When I think about it now, it makes my blood run cold. The things that *could* have happened! The house could have been wrecked. There was no way I was old enough to control a crowd of boys I hardly knew. But I didn't know at the time and I managed to convince my parents it would be okay. Looking back, all three of us must have been mad. I wouldn't dream of holding a party here on my own now. If I were having one, I'd hire a hall where I didn't have to worry about someone getting sick on the carpet. You can get a lot older and wiser in a year.'

SIXTH-FORMERS – AT SCHOOL AND COLLEGE

Mark:
'I get on great with my old man. We can have a conversation without either of us getting too involved. But my Mum is just too interested in me. If I state an opinion she wants to know why I feel that. If I've been somewhere she wants every little detail. If I mention a friend she wants to know his life story. It's sort of claustrophobic.

'I'm a get-up-and-do-it sort of person, not a deep thinker and she makes every conversation an ordeal. She gets really mad at me sometimes, when I'm sarcastic or when I walk off in the middle of her talking. She hits me, usually with a roll of kitchen foil. I just laugh and tell her to grow up.

'I can't see the point of arguments. They are usually about something you have done and therefore cannot undo. You are either sorry or not, so what's the point of going over it. Rows are over quickly in our house. It's hard to sulk because people just laugh at you.

'I suppose they have been fairly easy-going with me – my older sisters certainly think I've had it easy. I can't remember ever being forbidden to go somewhere. From my early teens onwards they didn't lay down rules about what time I came home. The one thing they are hot on is reliability. If I say I am going to be somewhere at a certain time I have to be there, or it really hits the fan. I've never objected. It's taught me reliability. I'm always on time. I wish some of my mates had been taught the same lesson.

'Mostly my parents have let me learn by my mistakes. They advised me not to have my hair bleached but I did and they didn't try to stop me. I think it's the only way. If they forbid something, you are sure to do it.

'They nagged about me not doing well enough in school but I'm okay, just a bit laid-back. I'll get some A-levels and do a business studies course at a Poly. I know my capabilities.

'I don't remember either of my parents going into what you might call the facts of life. Any of my mates who were told at home reckoned they had trouble keeping a straight face. There would be the old man telling them all this stuff they'd learned in the playground five years before. Their parents waited till they were around 14. If you haven't found out by then you might as well forget it.

'My Mum told me that girls had periods when I was in Junior School. From time to time my parents give me little pep talks about contraception and "being careful". I think they know that my girl-friend and I have a sexual relationship; though I doubt if her parents do. I've no idea if they approve. I expect they see it as inevitable. It wouldn't bother me if they didn't. When we've been away with either family they put us in separate rooms and we go along with that. It's just courtesy really and they don't put a 24-hour guard on us, so why take a stand.'

Judy:
'My parents are funny about my friends. They don't like one person; someone else is a bad influence. They are liable to judge someone on the way they look or talk. I'm vague about who I am going out with and I don't bring anyone home I think they will disapprove of. It's easier sometimes just to lie – to say I'm going out with someone they find okay rather than someone they dislike. I don't feel guilty about lying, it's a kindness – it stops them worrying.

'I've always been aware that I'm the baby. I'm the last child left at home and my parents want to keep me there as long as possible. My brother is not at home now and my father is away a lot because of his work. Sometimes when I'm going out for the fourth night in a row and I'm leaving Mum sitting there by herself in front of the telly, I feel guilty. She'll say, "You ought to stay in and do some work – how can you pass your exams if you're out every night"? But I suspect what she means is; "I'm lonely, can't you stay in with me once in a while."

'It doesn't stop me going out, but I do try to get home reasonably

early some nights so that I can talk to her. It's nice to have somebody
to talk to about where you've been. Someone who is really interested I mean, and mothers are, aren't they? It can't be much
fun though, having to rely on other people telling you about
their social life for your entertainment. I think Mums get a rotten
deal.'

Janice:
'My 14-year-old sister gets away with murder. She goes where she
likes, comes home late. It's unbelievable how casual my parents
have become since my older sister and I were that age.

'Of course they were new to it with us. Also we grew up together
almost like twins, so they had double trouble. It's odd though, we
older ones have always been able to talk to Mum and Dad about
anything, yet our younger sister who has all the freedom finds it hard
to be open with them. I think it's a lot to do with her friends. She
goes round with a crowd who think it's cissy to talk to your parents.
A lot of kids are like that at 14.

'The way you behave depends a lot on the crowd you go around
with. Within this college, there are several groups, all identifiable to
the other students. I belong to the football group – no, I don't play,
but my friends and I go round with the boys who play football.

'There's a group who are into drink and drugs – all the things
parents worry over. We steer clear of them. It may sound snobby,
but they are not our kind. I don't believe that you "get into bad
company" or "get led astray" the way parents seem to think. It's a
decision you make yourself.

'When you are allowed to make decisions for yourself, you really
think about it. When your parents make them for you, you automatically rebel against them. Honestly, I think growing up is all
about decision-making. I remember that first time I felt like an
adult. It was nothing stupid like wearing make-up or getting a boy-
friend. It was when I chose my options for O-levels in the third
year.

'A lot of the boys and girls, by the time they get to Sixth Form
College, have a steady boy or girl-friend. Not all though; there are a
lot of platonic mixed groups here, crowds of boys and girls who are
good mates and go around together.

'Personally I've never had any hassle over boyfriends with my
parents. They didn't like them all and they'd tell me so, but it was
never "don't let him darken my door again". I think the worst thing
parents can do is make a big fuss over something – you know, don't
you dare smoke or I'll lock you in your bedroom for a week, that
sort of thing. You immediately rush out and buy a packet of

cigarettes to defy them, or on the grounds that, if they forbid it, it must be good. I think they should tell you where they stand, but not over-react.

'My parents have always been very open with us about sex though they have never actually told us the facts of life. There have always been books on the subject all over the house. I'm sure some of my friends think we're a very funny family! It's been up to us to read them, which of course we did. At least my older sister and I did. Our younger sister developed a very funny attitude. She didn't want to hear about it or read about it. According to her, she already knows everything. Her attitude made my parents more determined to sit down and talk to her, because she had obviously got some sort of hang-up.

'If I'd needed to go on the pill before I was 16, I'd have had no qualms about telling my mother. She would tell me why she disapproved, if she did, but she wouldn't have stopped me. As it happens, I don't think girls that age should be given the pill . . . I don't think they should be sleeping with their boy-friends, they aren't mature enough, it's trying to grow up too soon.'

Tessa:

'I can come and go as I please now, though my parents expect me to tell them where I am going and when I will be home, out of courtesy. I haven't always had that much freedom. I think there was a big change when I came to the Sixth Form College – as if they accepted I was grown-up. Before that, like all my friends, it was a constant round of interrogation: Where are you going? Who are you going with? Where have you been? Who was there? What did you do? It's really irritating, but all parents seem to do it. If they would just stop shooting questions at you, you'd probably tell them. You certainly won't if they keep nagging.

'The other irritating thing is being constantly tied to the clock. You go to a party and suddenly the clock strikes 10.30 and you have to rush off. It's embarrassing. You are always the only one who has to rush home. Or that's how it seems. It was only when I came here and started talking about it to other girls that I found out most of them were in the same position. Some of them would rather face the row when they got home late than face the humiliation of having to leave early like a little kid.

'When you get older you can see why your parents made the rules, that they are trying to keep you safe. I suppose, if you are honest, you can see their point of view when you are screaming and fighting against it but the last thing on earth you'd do is let them know. That would be giving in to the enemy. However stupid the argument when you look back, it's a battle of wills at the time. Parents never back down, so why should you?

'I think the worst thing they do is refusing to treat you as an equal and talk openly to you about feelings. I'm sure families where everything is open and above-board all through your childhood, don't have many problems when their kids reach their teens. I know a family where the mother had an abortion and the 9-year-old son knows all about it. They talk openly about it, the same as any other family event and he understands the whole thing. I think that's great – I couldn't talk easily to my mother about something like that even now.'

Natalie:
'We used to have screaming, noisy rows quite regularly, me and my Mum. My little brother used to clear out of the way for safety. We fought about everything. It would blow up over a tiny little disagreement and just snowball. Mostly it was about me wanting to lead my own life, and about financial things. If I wanted money to go somewhere or for clothes, I'd say everybody else has it, everybody else can go. It wasn't true, but it made her feel guilty, which was what I wanted to achieve.

'My parents divorced when I was 10. I played on the fact that Mum was on her own, and didn't have a man to back her up. My brother does it now and it annoys me to see him. You definitely get away with more if you haven't a father around. Not that I don't see my father. I've always seen him regularly. Sometimes my Mum used to ring him up in desperation and order him to do something with me because she couldn't cope. He'd ring me up and tell me to stop giving her a hard time, but I didn't take much notice.

'During my early teens, I disliked my mother a lot. I blamed her for the break-up of the marriage, though she hasn't remarried and my father has. I enjoyed visiting him and I let her know. He was the one who gave us the treats and the outings. She was the one who laid down the rules.

'Now I find it far easier to talk to my step-mother than either of my parents. She has a younger attitude and she accepts me. If I tell Mum and Dad something, I know they are going to disapprove, but my step-mother will be interested and talk it over.

'The problem is that there just isn't any honesty between parents and teenagers. Both sides are lying to each other or putting on an act most of the time. Parents are worse though – they start doing it from the time you are a little kid. If I have children, I am always going to tell them the truth.'

Danny:

'Mostly I get on okay with my parents. My older sister has always had more trouble and more rows than I have. She reckons they are pretty unreasonable, but I don't know. . . . Every couple of months though, something happens that causes a big row. They yell at me, I lose my temper and pull a couple of doors off the hinges or something.

'They leave me to cool down and then I'm expected to apologise and I get forgiven – till the next time. It's a set routine, happens regularly.

'It happened last week actually. My bike broke down and I had to push it all the way home in the dark. I was late, naturally, it's a long way. The minute I walk in the door, tired and frozen, my Mum starts moaning and then my Dad has a go. Why hadn't I phoned? They thought I was under a bus, etc. etc.

'Well I hadn't any money and I was too tired to go looking for phone-boxes, which should have been obvious. I started hitting everything in sight (things not people) and managed to pull the door off. They left me alone, I went to bed, and next morning my Mum told me my Dad was waiting for an apology. By that time, I was in a good mood, so I played along with it. All over, all forgiven.

'I don't know why I do it really, I don't do much else they can grumble about. I don't take drugs or get drunk or even go out very often. I have a part-time job, so I provide my own spending money. There's not a great deal to do around here, but it's better than when I was younger. Between 12 and 15, I spent all my time hanging around the streets or wandering in the park. All my mates were the same. There's just nothing boys that age can do. You can't go in a pub, the pictures are too expensive, the girls are all at home practising putting make-up on or something, and the older boys knock you about if you go to the youth clubs (they used to throw darts at us). No wonder there is so much vandalism. Breaking a window or spraying the walls with paint relieves the boredom for a few minutes.'

Marianne:

I don't live with my parents during term-time – I'm in lodgings – and the lack of freedom always comes as a shock to me every time I go home. My mother really does still expect to know what I'm doing and thinking. I know she wants to know if I am sleeping with my boy-friend. She won't come right out and ask, but she beats about the bush. I don't think she'd believe I'm not. She is a very religious, moral person, but so am I in my own way.

'The family I stay with have teenagers too. They are very much more liberal and open with their kids. Maybe it's because they are young-ish and not religious especially. My mother tends to see everything in religious terms and it means that her mind is closed to new attitudes.

'My first boy-friend, when I was 14, was older than me. I knew the age difference worried her and I knew why – because he was sexually more sophisticated. If she'd admitted that, we could have talked about it, but she wouldn't. She would just look disapproving and worried and insist I was home by 10.30 p.m. To be fair, she didn't demand I gave him up. She just let me discover for myself that we didn't have a lot in common. It just died a natural death in the end.

'My mother tends to read stories in the papers and assume all young people are doing whatever is hitting the headlines – drug-taking, promiscuity, the pill, whatever. As if we are all going to latch on to the trendy vice! It doesn't work like that. In the last year at school, a lot of girls were sleeping with their boyfriends. Those of us who weren't would listen to their stories in the playground with eyes like saucers, but it didn't send us out to jump into bed with the first boy we met.

'I think, basically, we were more intelligent. We felt it was something to save for later, when we were mature enough to understand the emotions involved. And also I think we could see through to the reasons. A lot of the girls didn't sound as if they were doing it because of some great urge or even as if they enjoyed it. It was a way of getting attention, being one-up on the rest of us. Teenagers can suss each other out. We're not as gullible as adults believe.'

Annie:
'My mother and I have had some real stand-up battles. Usually over me going out too often or going to some club she didn't approve of. Sometimes I'd just storm out and go whatever she said; other times I'd storm up to my room and cry, instead.

'I think mothers really get the worst of it. Fathers aren't always there to see you at your worst. My father tends to blame my mother for everything I do wrong. She is the one I shout at when I'm angry because she is the one who is there.'

Julie:
'My parents are quite young. My Mum is 38. It makes a big difference. I can tell them anything I'd tell a friend. If I have a problem I'll talk to them, Mum in particular. I gossip to her all the time. If I've been to a party and people have been smoking pot, I'll

tell her. I tell her when I miss lectures. I told her when I was smoking. She'd never say, "Oh, you bad girl" or anything daft. If she doesn't think it's a great idea, she'll tell you why, then leave you to make up your own mind.

'I am influenced a great deal by what they say. I fancied being a beautician, but they think that's not good enough, not a proper career. So maybe I'll try something in the art world. What I'd really like is to get married and have children, but you've got to have a career before you get married. It's expected of you really and you'll need to work when the children are older. I'd live with someone, but only if we were hoping to get married. I think it's a good way of finding out if you are suited. I don't believe in having children outside marriage though. It's not fair on them.

'Come to think of it, I don't believe there's much I'd do, that my parents wouldn't have done 20 years ago. We're not very different.'

Joe:
'My father and I haven't got on for two or three years now. He was okay when I was a kid, but only because I didn't do anything he objected to. As soon as I developed a mind of my own, that was it. My mother is in the middle, torn between the two of us. Sometimes she is on my side, sometimes on his. He is always against me.

'She's okay my mother. I feel sorry for her and a bit guilty about the position she is in. I think some of the problems between me and my father stem from competition for her attention. He's jealous of the time she spends with me.

'It's not only that though. I'm an only child and my father has certain rigid expectations of how I should act, based on his own church-going background and how the children of his friends behave. He never thinks of me as an individual with my own personality.

'His idea of a teenager is someone who is very active, running and jumping and riding horses. I'm not a bit like that. I couldn't fulfil his expectations, so he tried to force me to. For a couple of years, around the age of 15 to 16, there was permanent confrontation in our house, rows day and night.

'What did he object to? Everything. He didn't like my friends. They were a bad influence on me. They were usually older than me and out of work. Having friends around is very, very important to me. I wasn't going to give them up. For a while I tried a dual existence, putting on an act to please him at home, never being myself there. In the end it got too awkward to keep up.

'In the past year I've tried harder to see my parents' point of view and I think they have made an effort at compromise. Their meaning of the word isn't mine though. They think it means talking me into doing it their way.

'I suppose you could say I've seen the light. I have started to look ahead and I don't want to end up at 25 with no qualifications and no job prospects like some of my friends. I failed my O-levels through messing around so I'm taking them again – and working this time. I won't let my parents change me or my way of life though. Why should I? I'm having a good time at the moment. I'm enjoying life.

'I understand how my father feels, what a disappointment I must have seemed in his eyes. But you've got to think of your own interests. It's your life.

'The biggest mistakes parents make are not seeing their children as they really are, as individuals – and not talking to them. They lay down rules and refuse to discuss them. I don't know why they won't talk to you. I suppose they see it as a sign of weakness, the first step on the slippery slope to losing control.'

Moira:
'I think it's been easier for me having two older sisters. My sisters say Mum and Dad have changed a lot over the years. They got the brunt of the arguments. By the time I reached my teens, our parents were more easy-going – or just worn down.

'Apparently it used to be different. My Dad once followed my sister into a pub, found her sitting with a pint of Guinness in front of her and ordered her home in front of her friends. I go out when I want to. My only complaint is that they worry too much about me and that makes me feel guilty. Mum will wait up for me even if I don't get in till 2 or 3 in the morning. It's stupid, because I'm fairly sensible. I can look after myself.

'I don't think they have really talked to any of us as teenagers. My middle sister says they didn't start to talk to her, as an adult, till she was married with children. It was as if she'd become someone they could understand at last, someone normal.'

Sally:
'My Mum is never grateful. If I hoover the floor, she won't say "Thank you" she'll say "Why didn't you wash-up as well?" Dad has two sets of rules, one for my brother, another for me. It's okay for my brother to go out where he fancies and stay out half the night. If I try to go out more than once a week, there's a row and I'm accused of treating the place like a hotel. What about equality?'

Gez:
'I have worse problems than most of my friends because my parents come from Italy. In their country nice girls do not go out with boys

or stay out late at parties, so they see no reason why I should do it here. At first I used to argue, then I realised that nothing I could say would change them.

'You have three choices. You go along with what they want, you go against them and have rows, or you tell lies. I lie. If I'm going somewhere they wouldn't approve of, I pretend I'm going to a friend's house. At home I behave the way they want me to be. Outside I do what I want. I don't like doing it, but I don't see I've got a choice.'

Ian:

'My parents keep trying to get me a Saturday job, although I don't want one. They think I should be earning my pocket money. I think I work hard enough at college and need my weekends off. A lot of parents are like that. It's a long time since they were at school and they have forgotten that it is hard work. I disagree with a lot of their views, but I don't say anything. There's no point.'

Charlotte:

'I don't understand why people have so much trouble. I agree with my mother on most things and I get on okay with my father. He doesn't interfere with what I want to do. I have two older brothers and if my parents were going to be shocked by adolescents they would have had plenty of time to get over it with them. I think the conflict only happens when parents are very set in their ways and not open to new ideas. The media blow up the idea of the generation gap. You can clash with people whatever their age – or you can get on well with them if you're lucky.'

Helen:

'Ours is a funny family. Mum and Dad are open about having favourites. Mum prefers my sister, Dad prefers me. He takes a great interest in everything I do and he gets ideas into his head about what I will do with my life.

'What he doesn't understand is that I am changeable. I get crazes. I know they won't last long, but Dad thinks they will be lifelong interests and starts planning a career for me around them. He wanted me to be a secretary. It came as a shock to him when I said I was going to be a P.E. instructor in the army.

'They both have a few strict rules. They don't like me going to night clubs; they are opposed to drinking under age. I had a spell a while ago when I had a different boyfriend every week. They worried then about what the neighbours would say seeing a different boy knocking at the door. "You'll spoil your reputation," they kept saying!

'Sometimes I stick out for what I want. I *am* going to be a P.E. instructor. Other times, if I know I'm not going to win I bend the truth a bit. I usually feel compelled to tell the whole truth afterwards though. They can't say anything then. Well, they can't *do* anything.

'I'm not perfect. I'm self-centred. I like to be noticed and I want the attention of my parents all the time. But parents aren't perfect either. If you can accept that you'll get on with them all right.'

18+ – OLD ENOUGH TO LOOK BACK

John, who comes from a small Northern mining town:

'I call my mother Mum, and my father by his first name. In a nutshell, that's the difference between the two of them for me. Now I'm older, my father is just another bloke, but she'll always be Mum.

'I think a lot of her. I'm going home on holiday soon and I've let the dyed streak grow out of my hair to please her. I'll get it done again when I get back.

'I've always been in on the trends. I've been a punk, had my hair striped, worn a scruffy old army coat and a greasy T-shirt. Not worth a second glance in a big city, but in a little place like ours, you cause talk.

'My parents hate anything like that, but they never tried to force me to conform. They just chuntered on and on about how bad I looked, which gets on your nerves more really. The thing that worried them most though was me and my brother turning into left-wing revolutionaries and joining picket lines and meetings. They thought we might get arrested or beaten up.

'Sex doesn't exist in our house. I suspect my mother might be a virgin! When they've been away and I've had a lass in, they always know, but they never come right out and say; it's just hints. It's not a subject fit to be mentioned, you see. The only time it has been, indirectly, was one morning when I got home with the milkman, after spending the night with a girl. I met my Dad on the doorstep and he said, "I don't want you getting that girl a name." Nothing more.

'It's always the girls they worry about, not me. My mother thinks I'm breaking some poor girl's heart every week. I should be so lucky! She's always hoping I'll find a steady girl and get engaged. A while ago, I broke off with a girl Mum liked – and I didn't dare tell the old dear for ages. I even persuaded the girl to pretend we were together when she met my Mum.

'It's not exactly that I'm afraid of my mother, but I suppose I want to keep the old dear's good opinion. Not enough to settle down yet though. Lasses (plenty of them), music and drink are what life's about when you're young.'

Lee, 18 years old, hair two-tone, ears pierced, arms tattooed, shoes pink, style trendy:
'My parents drive me mad. I'm an only child and they spend all their time trying to run my life. "Where are you going? When will you be home? Who are you going with?" Questions, questions – and rows when I won't answer them. And I believe all the suspicion is because of the way I look.

'Okay, I like to look different. I enjoy people looking at me. My friends are the same, only more so. Some of the guys wear make-up and high heels, but only when they go out at night. My Dad doesn't understand it's fashion. He takes one look and says: "My God, my son's a queer."

'Well, I'm not and neither are most of the lads in lipstick and eye-liner. Does it matter, anyway? The important thing in life is to be yourself. The way you dress expresses your personality. It doesn't change what you are inside. My Dad finds it really hard to equate the job I'm doing, with mentally-handicapped people, and the way I dress off-duty.

'He's ashamed of me. When I go out dressed up, he tells me not to talk to anyone he knows. The first time I upset him was when I was 14 and had my hair dyed green. I told him I was going to do it, but he didn't believe it till I walked in. Dad went mad. He knocked me about, but it was too late to change it.

'Then I had my arms tattooed. That I do regret. I don't want to be categorised with the blokes who wear tattoos, but I'm landed with them. There's a time and a place for everything. I don't come to work in my more outlandish gear. It would give people a certain impression and possibly lose me my job. But isn't it a pity older people only look skin-deep, and don't see the person underneath?

'They'd probably never think that I'm dead against drugs. I don't condemn people who take them, but it's sad they have to get their kicks that way. I do enjoy a drink. All my mates have been boozing for years. It's not half as much fun now we're legally old enough.'

Marc, student nurse:
'My parents are separated and I live with my Mum. It's easier with just one parent, especially now my sister is not living at home. My mother and I are more like a couple of flatmates now.

'She never tells me what to do, but then she never has. I can't remember ever being told to get home at a particular time. She didn't even insist on knowing where I was going. I didn't take advantage of the trust though, because I didn't want to lose it. The teenagers I've known who've played up the most are the ones who have had a tight régime at home. It stands to reason. You won't rebel if you've nothing to rebel against.

'Mum never tried to keep me a little kid, like a lot of mothers do. The opposite if anything. I was sort of a late developer. I've only ever had one girlfriend. I think my Mum worried that I wasn't behaving as badly as a teenager should and that I didn't even look the part.

'It was her who insisted I wear trendy clothes when I was 15. She took me to the pub with her and introduced me to drink, and from the time I reached 16, she would give me cigars to smoke on special occasions, like Christmas. I have to act manly and smoke them, even though they make me feel sick. I think maybe she's worried that I have missed a man's influence!'

Beverly, student nurse:
'I've had as much freedom as anyone could want since I was 13. I used to go round with a crowd who were into heavy metal and motor-bikes – the kind of boys mothers faint at – but because my brother was in the same gang, my parents never turned a hair.

'They were probably right. My friends used to envy me my freedom, but whereas the restrictions made them break out and experiment, the total freedom has made me quite old-fashioned and moralistic.

'My mother was pregnant and married in her teens – after a very strict upbringing – and I think she's tried to do things the opposite way round with me. I can talk to her about anything now, but she never actually told me about sex. She just seemed to assume I always knew!

'My father doesn't say much, but when he does, it's like God speaking. I don't necessarily do what Mum says, but I usually do what Dad says. When I was 15, he hit me – the only time ever. I understand why he did it. I was getting obnoxious, completely out of control. I would pick fights, answer back and be disagreeable just for the sake of it. I suppose he decided it had to be nipped in the bud, and it worked.

'There's only one thing I row with him about – equality. He expects me, like my mother, to do the washing-up or make the tea, while he and my brother sit gawping at the telly. He'll say, "Why don't you do some work around here? Why don't you tidy the house up?" as if it's my God-given duty. I just say "Why don't you?" It's one area where I won't let him bully me.'

Sandra, who is training to be a teacher:
'The rows started when I was 12. By the time I was in my mid-teens, I hated – there is no other word for it – my mother. There were several reasons: a personality clash for a start. In our house, my mother rules with an iron hand. She is very strong-willed. Dad hardly gets a look in.

'There are four of us, all girls and I'm the oldest, so maybe it's to be expected I'd have the roughest time. But I've noticed with the others that it's the stronger-willed ones, the ones who refuse to let Mother run their lives, who have the worst adolescent battles. I think what my mother finds hardest is no longer being allowed to plan and run our lives as she did when we were children.

'In my case, she's simply refused to trust me. You name it, she suspected I was up to it. She never accused me directly, but when I got home after a night out, she was always waiting, full of snide insinuations. I have a hot temper too and there was always a row.

'I've been expected to say where I was going right up till I left home. Quite often she would check up on me. If she had any doubts, she was not above driving round to a friend's house or a party to check I really was there. If I was late home, she'd lock me out.

'When I first came to college, she would ring me up and demand to know what I was doing at weekends. I just refuse to tell her now and refuse to let her rile me. Before I go home, I always ring and warn her, so she can get control of herself. If I walk in unexpectedly, all the anger she's been saving up for me just erupts. I'm like a red rag to a bull.

'I'm sure there are a lot of undercurrents in the relationship, like jealousy. My mother is no longer the belle of the ball, my sisters and I are young and attractive. Perhaps she also thought of me as a test case. If I got away with anything, the others would try it on too.

'Ironically, all those years while she was following me around, I was behaving myself. My convent school education and the commandments she'd drummed into me saw to that. What a pity she didn't know her own strength.'

Gavin, a university student:
'I suppose the worst thing my mother has ever done is embarrass me by talking about my funny little ways to neighbours when I was about 15.

'And I hate it when parents try to join in conversations with you and your friends and adopt this youthful tone that sounds so false. In your early teens, you're frightened to death about your friends meeting your parents in case they think they are awful and it reflects on you. As you get older, you realise that your friends are not auditioning your parents, and that their own are as bad anyway.

'My mother and I are more like friends now. I've seen her through two nervous breakdowns, so I feel I know her pretty well. My father is different. You couldn't have a close relationship with him. He keeps everything to himself. My older brother, Mike, and I spent years trying to guess what he was feeling. I don't think Mike ever sussed him out. I learned from Mike's mistakes. I learned to play the system.

'Mike was never interested in school work and my parents handled him wrongly. They pushed him too hard and stamped out what spark of enthusiasm for learning he had. They nearly did the same to me, though I'm bookish by nature. The problem is that what parents see as encouragement is actually nagging, and they keep on till you hate the sight of books. They don't value kids for what they are, only for what they want them to be.

'Anyway, Mike just stopped talking to them. They lost his trust. When he dropped out of college, they were the last to know. They found out because his tutor rang up to ask where he was. He'd been having problems keeping up with the work for two years and never said anything at home. He never came home to live after that.

'I learned that if I kept my head down and my nose to the grindstone, I could get out, via university. My father is a true Victorian, a total disciplinarian. He has no qualms about hitting his flesh and blood. When I was 13 or 14, he used to regularly wipe me round the hall. He had superior strength, so I learned to lie and put on an act to survive.

'He has no hard feelings towards me now. I've done what he wanted Mike to do. I don't expect he realises I've done it despite him, not because of him.'

BREAKING AWAY

Alison, 18 years old, unemployed, and living in a girls' hostel:
'I left home a year ago because I got bored with it and sick of the rules and regulations. My Mum and Dad treated me like a kid. My friends were all staying out till midnight and I was expected to be home by 10.

'It wasn't that I was going places they disapproved of. I'm not the night club type. Mostly it was just a crowd of us going round to one of our houses, playing records and having a drink and a laugh.

'I'm not an angel but I've never been interested in drugs. I've never sniffed glue, or even fancied it. But my family live on a big council estate and I knew a lot of kids who did. The minute my Dad heard it was going on, he assumed I was doing it too. Whatever I said, he wouldn't believe me; he preferred to believe what the newspapers said. That's what really cheesed me off in the end – the way they never trusted me. I mean, you live with them for 17 years and they don't even know you.

'The other problem was my older brother. He was worse than both my parents put together for bossing me about. He's on the dole, so he'd be there when I got home from school and during the holidays, laying down the law about which television programmes I could watch (the ones he wanted) and whether I could speak or play my records. My Mum would just let him walk all over me, my two sisters and my other brother. He got all the sympathy just because he couldn't find a job.

'My other brother wouldn't stand for being bossed around and they were always fighting. I shared a room with my two sisters. There was no privacy and we all got on each other's nerves.

'I walked out after a row and went to stay with my friend. I rang and told Mum I wasn't coming back. She just said "Suit yourself". Mum hated my friend. She blamed her for putting ideas into my head, which was ridiculous because I am – and was – old enough to make up my own mind. A lot of parents are like that. When you do something they don't like, they say it's your best friend's fault.

'I didn't cut myself off from the family or anything. I've kept in touch. I go round to see them nearly every Sunday. After a while, when they realised I was serious and that I was able to survive without them, they just accepted it. My Mum has more or less agreed that me leaving was for the best. At 17 or 18, it's no big deal having a life of your own, is it? It's natural.

'Dad has never told me how he feels. He didn't make a fuss and try to get me back or anything. I don't think he's bothered. I'm not his favourite; my older sister is. He acts like he has no feelings, but when she leaves, it's really going to hurt him.'

Brigitte, a fragile, pretty girl; carefully made-up, and looking older than her 17 years. She lives in a hostel and is out of work after finishing a government scheme. She was looking after her baby half-sister, the child of her 37-year-old mother's second marriage:

'My Dad left 9 years ago. We never see him. Mum brought us up alone, all five of us. It was great. She was really easy-going, but loving too. We hardly had any rules and regulations. She went out quite a lot herself, so we had a great deal of freedom.

'Till she married my stepfather, that is. Then it all changed. We quite liked him when they were just going out together, but after he moved in he was different. He wanted to rule the roost. He didn't want us going out at night – but he also didn't seem to want us staying in. We got under his feet and made noise. The truth is he just didn't like us.

'The first to go was my elder sister. He said it was time she left home. At first Mum took our part, but then she seemed to go round to his way of thinking. She told us that once we were 16, we were grown-up and she wanted no more responsibility for us.

'I moved out – well, I felt I'd been pushed really – and went to stay with this man who used to baby-sit for us. Not a boy-friend or anything. He was 50, more like a father. Trouble was, he started to act like he was *my* father, telling me where I could and couldn't go and who with. So I moved into this hostel. There's more freedom here. They treat you like a grown-up, but what I really want is a flat, which I can share with my best friend.

'We've put our name down for a council flat. We know we'll have to wait a couple of years. We're saving a bit from our dole money every week for furniture. We don't want to have wild parties in the flat or anything. It would just be nice to have a place of your own and the freedom of come and go as you please without someone telling you what you should be doing. If I had a job as well, I'd be really happy, but I don't see much chance of that.

'I'm looking after the baby for two weeks because my mother is expecting another soon and she needs a bit of help. She rang up and asked me. I only hear from her when she wants something. I suppose she's happy with her new family, but I didn't ask her. It's not a very nice thing to say, but I don't care about my mother at all. I used to love her, but she's not an important part of my life any more.'

Michael. Like a sizeable number of homeless young people in English cities, he is Scottish. He is unemployed in England as he was at home, but remains convinced that there are more prospects this side of the border. 'There are better prospects anywhere than in Glasgow!'

He is 17, intelligent – he has 7 O-levels – and polite. His clean shirt and cords suggest that he is very capable of looking after himself, and he carries none of the weary disenchantment of the homeless unemployed. To be accurate, Michael is no longer homeless. After enduring a spell in a night shelter, a welfare organisation rented him half a house – he shares with another young man.

He is mature and you are left with the impression that despite family problems and high unemployment, leaving home for Michael was just a part of growing up:

'I grew up very suddenly at 15. For me that was the point at which teenage rebellion for the sake of it came to an end. My parents are divorced. There's only Mum at home. I came home from school, one afternoon expecting her to be in the kitchen getting my tea. She wasn't. She was upstairs lying half-in and half-out of bed, unconscious.

'I couldn't bring her round, so I rang for an ambulance. She had a lot of tranquillisers and sleeping pills from the doctor and she'd taken an overdose. Accidentally I think . . . I hope. I felt very bad – guilty, I suppose. My older brother had just been sent down for five years, and apparently she was in the process of having a nervous breakdown. I hadn't noticed.

'I'd noticed she was getting short-tempered and shouting at me for nothing. I thought she was turning into a real old nag. I'd pack my bag and stay at my mate's house to let her cool down. Sometimes I'd walk out of the house and she'd be sitting in a chair, just staring at the wall. Two days later I'd get back and she'd be in the same place, same position. She was hardly moving or eating, just making the occasional cup of tea. She was also taking 6 or 7 pills a day, but she didn't tell me. I'd no idea till I found her unconscious. You don't think at 15.

'I suppose I believed my mother was indestructible till then. I think I grew up overnight. Before she went into hospital, I'd been fairly wild. I'd had a lot of older friends, guys I'd met through CB radio. Girls too – I was dead keen on older women around 20!

'I used to spend my nights in the pub or night clubs getting as drunk as I could. I'm big, so I could get in without questions. I had a Saturday job on a building-site to pay for my social life. When my Mum came out of hospital, I stayed in and helped her round the house. She let me do it till she was up and about, then she said it wasn't my job.

'She's always believed that helping in the house is not men's work. Both my brother and I were brought up to be chauvinist pigs. I can cope with my washing and house-keeping, no bother, but if there was a woman around, I'd let her do the lot.

'My mother is old-fashioned in some ways, quite modern in others. She's always been very open about sex. She'd explain anything. Even when I was 14 or 15, she'd give me little talks and I'd have to say, "Mum, please, I *know*." On the other hand, she didn't want me to put it into practice, at least not in her house.

'I couldn't walk in past her and take a girl up to my bedroom. I know lads who can. She had a fairly unrealistic idea of my relationships with girls. She thought I was innocent, and I played up to it.

'The sort of girls I like are punks, the weirder they look and dress the better. My mother's idea of the right girl is a sweet-natured little thing with a pony tail and white socks who fitted in with her ideas. Well, she has enough problems without me giving her more.

'My brother for instance. If I told you the details of his life, you'd think I was talking about a hardened criminal. But he's not. Everyone likes him. He's very kind-hearted. Most of the scrapes he's been in have happened by accident or bad luck. Once you've been in trouble with the police, they know your face and you're always the first suspect.

'He was fine till the family split up, when he was 12. After that he started getting into trouble. It wasn't easy being his younger brother. You felt the teachers and the police were watching your every move, waiting for you to go off the rails. Worse, I felt my mother was. I've never been interested in a life of crime though.

'I suppose it was one of the reasons I left, to get away from being watched. And then I've always been a bit of a wanderer, packing my bags during school holidays and taking off with a mate for a week's camping. My mother has always understood. She's never tried to tie me down.

'Then there's work. I don't want to be a permanent drop-out. The only job I've ever had was in a supermarket. I got it, not for my exam results, but because I was big enough to carry big boxes around. A lot of people have told me I can get into college here, get some A-levels and maybe go on to the Polytechnic.

'I'll probably do something about it next year. Just at the moment, I'm enjoying being independent, having no pressures. I can survive on my dole money. I mean, life is what you make it, even life on the dole.'

PART TWO

Parents

1

Just a stage they're going through!

'They were a happy family once . . . Then last year, when Jeffrey turned fourteen and Matilda twelve, they had begun to change; to grow rude, coarse, selfish, insolent, nasty, brutish and tall . . . the children she loved had turned into awful lodgers – lodgers who paid no rent, whose leases could not be terminated.'

Alison Lurie *The War Between The Tates*

It's one of life's ironies that at the time teenagers are at their most problematic, parents, those supposed pillars of strength and reason, are going through a funny stage themselves. They are liable to be battling their way through their mid-life crisis.

Thanks to the Americans who go in for such things, the mid-life crisis is a fairly well-documented phenomenon. Somewhere between the mid-thirties and the mid-forties, we all do a bit of stock-taking and re-appraising of our lives. However depressing the thought, we become aware that from here the rest of the trip is downhill. If you've got energetic and attractive young people around the house, you're all the more conscious of it. It's a time when, for a spell, a lot of people become obsessed with the process of ageing, and the number of comparatively young (i.e. middle-aged) people they see dying around them.

Men (or career women) now have a clear view of how far up the ladder they will go. Success is no longer just around the corner. They know at what point, career-wise, they will finish. Chances are it's a long way from the position they dreamed of at 20. Even if they have soared to the top of their particular tree, there's often a feeling of anti-climax – is this all there is?

There is an ever-present awareness that time is running out, and they have to decide if the life they have is the one they really want. And if not, whether they should opt out, whoever gets hurt in the process, and do something more satisfactory. This watershed has been called the male menopause.

It's not unheard for a man to opt out of his safe job and family commitments. He may even opt out of his marriage – it's a flash point for ego-boosting affairs. Gauguin went off to paint dusky beauties in the South Seas. The fictional Reginald Perrin faked suicide and tried to become a different person. On the other hand a man in mid-life may start to regret that he has missed out on basic things like family life. He may turn back towards the family he has neglected emotionally for years, whilst he was pouring his energy into his career and other out-of-house activities.

And if he does, what does he find? That instead of waiting breathlessly for Daddy's attention, the children have grown into stroppy adolescent strangers, who want none of this togetherness.

'I often wonder what happened to the lovely little girl who used to live here,' said one such father wistfully, watching his 14-year-old punk daughter disappear into the distance. 'I think a wicked fairy swapped her for that strange young lady when I wasn't looking.' He was only half-joking.

At the very time a man starts truly to value his family, his children are busily breaking the ties one by one. He may also, for the first time, envy his wife her humdrum, home-based life. She will have had the opportunity to grow close to their children. She has had a side of life he has missed.

'Women grow strong in middle-age,' said Peter Houghton, founder of The National Mid-Life Centre. 'I believe that the first half of life belongs to men, but the second half belongs to women.'

A pretty thought, but is it true? Woman, 40, also has her problems. If she is still attractive she may be jealous of her pretty teenage daughter and try to compete with her. (Fathers often do the same with sons.) If she had her children late, she may already be facing the physical problems of the menopause when they get to adolescence.

Either way, she too realises with a jolt that life is short, and whatever she wants to do, it's now or never. Hence the last-chance babies, the number of 'late beginners' who enrol at Institutes of Higher Education to train for the profession they discarded in favour of motherhood. And the women who set out to find a lover–often, of late, a younger man.

Which brings us to another sensitive point. Men in middle-age tend to suffer from reduced potency, partly caused by psychological factors. Peter Houghton again: 'Don't ever assume that men are less bothered than women about the ravages of age: the paunch, the thinning hair, the wrinkles. I know men who are reduced to impotence by revulsion at their own middle-aged bodies.'

Sexually, couples may have drifted apart anyway, once their children were in early adolescence. 'They are so knowing, so dirty-minded, and so plainly disgusted at the thought of "old people" doing anything sexual,' said the 39-year-old mother of three teenagers. 'In the end, you are too embarrassed to bother.'

The other major marital shock comes when the children leave home – or are there in name only because of frantic social lives. At this stage parents who have drifted apart and probably have nothing in common except the children are forced to get to know each other again. They have to learn to talk to each other and organise their lives as a couple for the first time in 15 or 20 years. Some don't make it. They find they have nothing left. Mid-life is a flashpoint for divorce.

A woman who has been entirely home-based for decades, whether she is married or on her own, has yet another crisis to face – the much-feared Empty Nest Syndrome. If you have devoted your whole life to bringing up children, virtually living through them, what have you left when they depart?

'I'm trying to train myself for life without him,' the mother of an 18-year-old only child told me. 'I go away for occasional weekends with my husband and leave Alan behind, but I find myself thinking or talking about him 90 per cent of the time I'm away.'

For some women, it takes a lot of searching to find a substitute for full-time motherhood. Some hang on grimly, treating their long-grown, long-flown children like babies at every possible opportunity, still living through them.

But that's not the reaction of all women. There are those, who, once they have decided (or nature has decided for them) that child-bearing is no longer a possibility, get a surge of energy for other things.

For many a middle-aged man, his wife's new-found urge to get out into the big wide world just as he is turning towards domesticity is another bone of contention.

'My husband is jaded with work, but it's a joy to me to get up each morning and come into the office,' explained one 45-year-old woman from behind the reception desk of a plumbing company. 'It's the novelty value of it I suppose, and being appreciated and told I'm doing well for a change.'

There's life on the other side of the mid-life crisis, and indeed, the changes it has wrought may be small, internal ones, only visible to the mind's eye. But they are inevitable – the personality changes, the relationship changes and the occasional scar. As Gail Sheehy puts it in *Passages – Predictable Crises of Adult Life*: 'The consensus of current research is that the transition into middle life is as critical as adolescence and in some ways more harrowing.' Tell that to your teenagers when they are hogging all the attention!

In these days of equality, it grieves me to say, fathers are different. From mothers that is. Not being so close to their children on a day-to-day basis, they rarely see the worst, and they expect more from them. They are more likely to expect their daughters to be virgins, and their sons to be sexually advanced (but responsible!) Macho Men.

More secrets are kept from them, either through fear or excessive respect. 'I might tell my mother, but never, ever my father,' is a sentence I heard regularly.

It was harder to get fathers to talk about their teenagers. They left it to their wives, or left the room, or said things like, 'We've had no trouble with ours. They are good kids really,' while their wives gulped in disbelief. Dennis, quoted here, started the interview with just those words, then slowly went on to tell the hair-raising, heartbreaking story of life with his eldest daughter.

'It's just,' he explained at the end, 'that I'm not in the habit of thinking about my kids or trying to understand them. Quite honestly, they've always been a mystery to me.'

2

Parents talking

STARTING OUT AS YOU MEAN TO GO ON (parents of young teenagers)
In some ways mothers and fathers have to learn all over again to be
parents when their children reach adolescence. They have to brush
up on skills and virtues such as flexibility, diplomacy, mind-reading,
negotiating ability, how to lose an argument gracefully, and – as a
psychologist put it – 'not to take their children's behaviour so
personally'. The lessons are harder for some than for others.

Denise, Mary, Ray, Janet and Alan, the first interviewees live on
a large council estate where there is a high rate of teenage pregnancy, vandalism and petty crime (a situation certainly not improved by unemployment). For conscientious parents, like those
interviewed, this breeds a special determination that their children
will not, as one put it 'join the riff-raff that give us all a bad name.'

Denise, mother of two teenage girls, Sharon (15), Teresa (14) –
and a younger daughter:
'I can honestly say we've had no problems in our family. They have
been brought up in a loving, open family – not one where certain
subjects like sex are taboo, as it was in my family.

'We have strong moral standards, but we want them to understand that sex is all right as part of a loving relationship – it's not
something dirty. Paul will give me a cuddle at home and the girls will
say "Dad's after his nookie again".

'We can watch television together and if there's something – well,
questionable – we can talk about it. I know a 13-year-old boy who
cannot see a couple kissing on the screen without going beetroot
with embarrassment. What sort of attitude is he going to grow up
with?

'I find television is a very good starting-point. If there is some item
on VD or something, I'll say to the girls "Do you know what that
means?" If not, I'll tell them.

'We go out a lot as a family. I go to discos with them – church and
school functions, not the nightclub variety, which fortunately they
aren't interested in anyway. I make an effort to keep up-to-date
with their interests and musical tastes. The other day I bought them
some singles – and managed to pick the ones they would like. That's
a bit of an achievement for a Mum.

'One disagreement we have had was the noise level of their tapes and records. We solved it by getting them headphones. It's just a case of working out the easiest way of living together, whatever your age.

'We don't treat them like children. They had a party recently and they made it clear they didn't want only soft drinks. So we got some cider and mild and went out for the evening. Everybody was very responsible. There were no problems. It's all about trust. You've got to trust your children and generally, they'll repay that trust.

'Only one thing really worries me – their physical safety. I don't let them walk alone at night, or hang about in the streets with their friends. That sort of thing was okay when we were teenagers, but nowadays the streets are dangerous. It means we fetch and take them everywhere.

'The only thing that irritates me is their casual assumption that money grows on trees. They'll ask for a computer for a birthday present or a video-recorder. How easily those words drop from their lips. All I ever got was some sweets or a couple of oranges or a doll if I was really lucky. But all their friends have them, so you go without yourself so they won't be different.'

Mary, married to Ray, has a 14-year-old daughter Tina, and a 13-year-old son Wayne:
'Wayne is a child still, but Tina – she could be three or four years older than him. Girls grow up very early these days. She feels she is old enough to go out where she pleases, have a boyfriend, to run her own life, virtually. That's the crux of the problem. We married young – sometimes I feel if I were older myself, not so able to identify with her, I'd be better able to handle her. There are times when I feel almost as young as she is, she acts so grown up on the surface.

'I think teenagers need rules, they need to know how far they can go – and they keep on pushing you a little further. On the other hand if you lay down the law too rigidly, they get to a stage where they hate you. You tell Tina to be in by 8 o'clock, she will try to make it 8.30. Make it 8.30 and you'll be ringing round to find her at 9 o'clock. She came in the other night and I yelled at her, "I'm sick of you coming in late". She yelled back, "I'm sick of *being* late". There's no answer to that! Does she think it's our fault?

'I don't think they tell parents everything. You'd be stupid to think they did. They will tell you what they want you to know. Maybe if you are very lucky and very unusual, your son or daughter may never come up against something that they can't tell you, something they know you would disapprove of. Sometimes I think you are the last one they would tell if they had a problem. You are too close. I know there is something on my daughter's mind at the moment, something that is worrying her. I can sense it, I can even guess what it is. But there is no way I can force it out of her till she decides she wants me to know.'

Ray:
'You have to come down firmly and say, "That is it, not a minute later." I don't think they believe how you worry. From the moment your child goes out, there's a little niggling worry at the back of your mind. Every minute after the time they are supposed to be in that worry builds up. By the time they get in you're ready to explode so what they see is anger and bad-temper, not your fear for them.

'I suppose parents come to be associated with shouting and bad-temper. It's sad how the warmth and affection seem to go out of the relationship with your kids when they reach the teens. I mean the feelings are still there, you *want* to be affectionate to them, but you are afraid of being rejected if you try.

'There are some close moments when you least expect it. The other morning Tina said to me, out of the blue, "What would you do if you thought someone was two-timing you?" Well, you can't laugh. Those boy/girl things are very, very serious when you're that age, aren't they? So I had to sit down and think about something that hasn't occurred to me for a long time."

Mary:
'Their relationships with the opposite sex *are* serious – and that's one of the biggest worries. Tina goes out in a foursome – with her friend and their boyfriends – and they come back as a foursome. But I know they split into twosomes while they are out.

'They go to each other's houses, but that's as far as you can get. I say "What were you doing at your boy-friend's house?" and she'll say "Oh, dossing around". So you suggest she dosses around at our house and she says, "There's nothing to do at our house". You can't really get a satisfactory answer.

'Of course sex is thrown at them from all sides – films, newspapers, televison. Boy-friends were a long way from my mind at Tina's age. Pop stars pinned on the bedroom wall were the nearest I got. Now it's the real thing.

'I try to censor what they see. I won't have a video because I know the sort of films they can get – not hard porn or anything, just suggestive modern films. I try not to let them see anything I don't like the sound of, but you can't be sure when they are at someone else's house. Even worse, I'd heard there was nudity and sex in

Gregory's Girl and I refused to let either of them see it in the cinema. So what happens? – The school gets it in and shows it in the dinner hour at 10p a time to anyone who fancies seeing it. You can't fight that.'

Janet, mother of 14-year-old Beth and 13-year-old Mandy, plus two younger children; married to Alan:
'I'm the strict one. Alan thinks I'm hard on them. I do worry a lot because of what happened to me. You don't want your mistakes repeated. My mother never talked to me; she never told me anything. I found out the hard way.

'Beth was born when I was sixteen. The only time my mother spoke to me about sex was when I was three months' pregnant. She must have got wind of what was going on and she said to me one day, "Have you been naughty?" I said no, of course. When I went into hospital to have my baby, I didn't know how it would be born, where it would come out. That's how much I knew about my body.

'I've been very lucky. We have a teenage marriage that turned out happy. But you can't help but be affected by your experiences. My two girls are very different from each other. Beth is quiet and sensible, Mandy is cheekier and wants her own way. She's the one I worry most about. I trust Beth – well almost.

'We've left her at home alone with her boyfriend. It's the first time I've done it and it worries me. I told them my feelings before I left. I said, "Kissing and cuddling is all right, but no more. I don't believe in sex before marriage." It's the first time I've actually put it into words, though I'm sure the girls know how I feel. Beth agrees with me. So does her boyfriend – or so he said. I'm not sure how Mandy will feel when she gets a boyfriend.

'It's so hard for them to know what's right when they get these conflicting images all around. We live near a big comprehensive school. I can look out of my window and see boys and girls lying together on the grass in the lunch hour and after school. The school doesn't seem to feel it's their business. I really regret the passing of single-sex schools.

'I won't have newspapers in the house, except the evening paper, because of the rubbish that is in them; nor are Beth and Mandy allowed to watch television late at night. They go to bed – or at least up to their rooms – at 9 o'clock. Partly for their own benefit and partly, I'll be honest, because that is the only time in the day Alan and I get together. I think it's very important to get a bit of time together as a couple.

'If the girls go out at night, we escort them both ways. I don't go along with the view that it's the very protected ones who go astray, not as long as they have some knowledge. They get sex education at school, and at home you give them the moral education to go with it. I wouldn't agree to them going on the pill under 16 either – it's too young. What I hope they will do is wait till they are old enough to make adult decisions.

'I don't want my girls forced into an early marriage or an abortion or to end up like many of the young girls on this estate, unmarried and tied down with a baby at 16 or 17. They say that young girls deliberately have a baby, in order to get away from home and get a council flat, as there are no jobs for them. That's the worst thing I could imagine for my daughters.'

Alan, married to Janet:
Bringing up a girl is more worrying than having a boy. There's always this worry over sexual things. It's not an equal world. Girls get left with the consequences, so you are stricter on them.

'Just the same, I don't agree with my wife about everything. If Beth came to me and said, tomorrow, that she wanted to go on the pill, I'd agree. I'd think that the fact that she'd thought about it and got the confidence to approach me, meant she was mature enough.

'I had a different background to Janet, you see – my home was happier and more stable, as a teenager. It's when your kids are this age that your own family background starts affecting how you treat them.

'I think there comes a point when you realise that you have to live your own life, they have to live theirs and you have to force yourself to stop worrying.

Roger a lecturer, married to Ruth, a teacher. The oldest of their four children is 14-year-old Amy:
'My wife always said that Amy was my child, and Helen, the second one, was hers. Helen is more turbulent, Amy is rather controlled. I've always had very tender feelings about her. There are snapshots in my mind of her at different stages; toddling down the hospital ward when we went to visit her mother and baby sister.

'Of course things have had to change. She used to creep into our bed in the night or come in in the morning for a cuddle. She doesn't do that any more – well, she couldn't, could she? But I do miss that warmth and affection.

'There are areas of disagreement between Ruth and me on bringing up children. I started off as an educational under-achiever, relatively so anyway. I went to a public school, where my two brothers, both highly academic and athletic, had been before me. It was an awful lot to live up to and I couldn't, so I felt very rebellious towards the teachers and the system. Consequently, I don't put the store by paper qualifications that Ruth does. It's she who pushes Amy, and insists that she keeps up her 'cello and piano lessons, whatever other teenage delights are beckoning.

'What concerns me is *who* she will be, not *what* she will be. I hate the vapid, empty attitude of some young people. I was acutely lonely as a young person myself, so I am delighted that Amy has a large circle of friends of both sexes, and a good social life, even if it has turned me into a taxi service.

'At the moment her friendships with boys are platonic. I don't think I'm being naïve in saying that. I know it will not always be so. She wanted to finish lunch early the other day, so that she and some friends could go to see a boy off on the train. I felt myself getting irritated. Why was this boy more important than us?

'We hear there is another boy in the group who is keen on her and wants to take her out. I'm pleased she's popular, but there is a niggling feeling that no boy is good enough for her. I know I'll have to watch myself, not set ridiculous expectations. You don't want to be the traditional joke father.

'It's been interesting to me to see how strong the incest taboo is. I'm very much aware of the attractiveness of some of the lasses Amy brings home (a man doesn't look at a girl and see her with her brithdate stamped on her forehead!) I am also aware, objectively, that my daughter is an attractive young woman, but I don't look at her and register this, as I do with her friends.

'We never formally gave her sex education. Well, there are plenty of excellent books you can let them read. Her mother dealt with it, I couldn't. I was traumatised, you see, by my father calling me into his study at 13 and giving me what he took to be a talk on sex and was actually a lecture on pathology. It took me a long time to get over it.

'Parents feel guilty about not being able to chat matily to their teenagers about sex, but I wonder if it isn't part of the taboo imposed by nature and maybe a good thing. Perhaps we are meant to find it a bit embarrassing. Very few young people actually want to hear that sort of information from their parents. It's as embarrassing for them as for us.

'Perhaps the kindest thing parents can do is keep their nose out of that area. I hate the idea of parents marching their teenagers to the clinic to be put on the pill or providing a boy with a packet of contraceptives. It is prying into a very secret area and reducing the relationship to the sordid and the drab. Of course adolescents are sexual beings and are probably experimenting and experiencing feelings in a very rich way – but probably not the basic and crude way parents immediately assume. I'm sure adults can take a lot of the joy out of adolescent sexuality with their vulgarity.

Ruth:
'She is nudging us all the time towards more freedom. She no longer wants to come on family days out. She wants to stay out later and later. You can see that she's pushing towards the midnight curfew and outings to nightclubs. We just wouldn't let her go to places like that. We do not like the whole ethos of nightclubs. But every day now there are little – not arguments exactly – but discussions over every single thing. Maybe I should be glad they are not blazing rows, but then we are not the sort of people who fight. We discuss.

'One of the tricks is to force an instant decision. Can she do this? Her friends need to know *now*. I've learned not to be rushed. I insist we discuss it coolly. When I say no, she makes me feel a real pig. I said to her the other day, "I won't have this, you blaming me for spoiling your fun. I am not a bad mother."

Roger:
'We don't have a television set on principle. We didn't want them exposed to violence and blatant sex prematurely and it wastes so much time. Of course they do see it at friends' houses and Amy does have pop music on the wireless.

'It has caused me some heart-searching. I am aware of the affect being different can have on an adolescent among their friends.

'She does say to us sometimes, "I wish you were more like other people's parents." When you investigate what this means, it's something to do with having a busy social life and going to the pub regularly, instead of being on committees and the like. We tried this recently, planned a totally social night out at the theatre. Amy was to baby-sit. Then she complained because she wanted to go out on the same night.'

Ron, early forties, two children – Karen (14) and Andrew (12). He is an electrician:
'To me, the worst thing about teenagers is this anti-everything attitude. You know – "What a dump", when you take them somewhere. "What a Wally" for everyone over 30 – or even another teenager who dresses differently. Perpetual scorn and boredom with everything. They don't want to go anywhere or do anything. If you suggest going for a drive in the country, they look at you as if you are mad.

'I honestly can't remember being that jaded with life at that age. Going out on my bike with my father was a treat. A train journey was an exciting event. Maybe it's because they've seen it all now by the time they start school – if not first-hand, then on television.

'In one way I feel sorry for them, but it does make them a real pain in the neck. I think you've got to force them out of it, make them take an interest in the world around them, otherwise it becomes part of their character. They grow into bored, scornful people.

'The thing that amazes me is the total lack of respect they have for adults. There's no way my generation would have stood up to an adult and rubbished what they were saying. We cared too much for our health and well-being. We'd have got a sharp clout across the ear. Where do today's 13 and 14-year-olds get such over-confidence from?

'The young girls are even harder to understand than boys. Your daughter can turn overnight into a total stranger. Suddenly the pretty little girl is putting warpaint on her face, dying her hair a funny colour and wearing the most awful clothes – by the time she is 13. My daughter is a clever, pretty girl, who takes off her smart school uniform and deliberately turns herself into the biggest mess you ever laid eyes on. If you try to advise her, she says you have no idea what's fashionable. If you refuse to let her out looking like that, there's rows and days of sulking.

'My wife says I'm making a mountain out of a molehill, that she's just experimenting. But what area will she be experimenting in next if you give her free rein? Tarted up, she can look years older – expecially to the lads. I've already had to see one lad off. She was sneaking off to meet him. I told him I'd knock his head off. Then I told him that if he wanted to see her again he'd have to call round to the house and do his talking there. I suppose the steam coming out of my ears must have put him off that idea!

'I realize you can't lock them up, but I don't think a girl under 16 should be going out alone with a boy, even a lad her own age. I know what young lads are like. I was one. Maybe it's different if it's a boy you know and trust. But would I trust any of them – or my daughter? Could she withstand the pressure?

'All this stuff about giving them freedom and they'll find their own level is rubbish. It's a fact of life that teenagers will try and hoodwink their parents. The duty of the parents is to see they don't get away with too much. I will do everything in my power to keep mine on the straight and narrow. If they break the rules, they are punished, usually by withdrawal of privileges.

'Of course there have to be different rules for a boy and a girl, certainly where the opposite sex and freedom are concerned. Boys don't get pregnant. If, later on, I thought my son was sleeping with a girl, I'd warn him about the consequences – like the fact that he'd be expected to stand by her if she was in trouble, and that it's not the ideal way to start marriage. From then on it would be his problem. With my daughter, I'd do everything humanly possible to see she wasn't in the situation – including following her to check up.

'I don't believe in abortion and giving a girl of 14 or 15 the contraceptive pill is just obscene. It's like neutering a cat. "Take one of these daily and forget about morals or decency". That is opting out of parental responsibility.

'My wife's views are more lax than mine and it causes a lot of arguments. I feel we ought to present a united front. It's confusing for a child when you are saying different things, and the child will obviously pick the easiest touch. I feel that my wife gangs up with Karen against me, and at other times she uses me as the heavy to bring her to heel. I don't know whether she is, in fact, more liberal in her outlook, or whether she is just afraid of the kids not liking her if she enforces authority.

'My wife is inclined to excuse our daughter's behaviour as "Just a phase, the way kids are nowadays". But it is a vicious circle. The reason young people behave so badly is precisely *because* so many parents shrug their shoulders and give in. Just because a lot of people do something, it doesn't mean it's right.'

'I don't think I'm over-reacting. I work in a poor area of the city and I've watched young girls wind up pregnant at 16. . . .

'It's a slippery slope. It starts with them wanting to punch half a dozen holes in each ear, because "everyone does it". Then they *must* have their hair glued into spikes, and they *must* stay out till 2 a.m. at night clubs or they will feel deprived and their friends won't want to know them.

'You don't have to give in. You can put your foot down firmly, early, and keep it there. I mean, it's for their good you are doing it; it's because you want the best for them. Sooner or later they will realise that.'

'THERE'S ONE IN EVERY FAMILY' – black sheep, that is; the problem sons and difficult daughters. The majority of parents with no prompting, singled out one of their teenagers to talk about – the difficult one.

There were no hard and fast rules about which position in the family this child might occupy. He (slightly more were boys) might be the youngest, the oldest, the middle child or in one case, a twin.

What they had in common was finding growing up a traumatic experience. Their families were finding it no easier.

Paul, aged 46, married to a nurse, works in the Civil Service. He has two sons and a daughter, aged 16 to 19:
'I always thought it would be the younger boy, Simon, who would be the problem. Well, they say the middle child has to fight for attention, and I'd seen it with my brother caught in between two of us. Also Simon was a bit of a handful when he was young.

'But no, when the crunch came it was Tom, the studious one, who caused the worry, and who still does. He seemed to be a late developer, problem-wise. Simon worked through a lot of the rebellion when he was in his early teens, young enough for us to have control over him. But Tom waited till he was too old for us to tell him what to do.

'Not having any control over them, that's what bothers me. I like to know where my kids are and what they are up to. But you have no way of knowing, do you? What's Tom up to when he goes out at 10 p.m. and doesn't get home till 3 a.m.? He certainly never volunteers the information.

'There are so many pitfalls; drugs and the like. I promised myself I'd never be the sort of parent who browbeats his children, and I hope I've kept to that. But he does treat the house like a hotel and that annoys me. I don't know why it gets up my nose so much, exactly. Maybe it's envy. I have to say where I'm going and get home at a reasonable hour or there will be rows with my wife. But my son is answerable to no-one. I suppose I envy him that freedom from responsibility, and having life and youth and so many opportunities still before him.

'I also get frustrated because I can't make him grab hold of those opportunities, the way I feel he should. You see, I never had those opportunities. I left school at 15, and had to work my way up, every step of the way, getting my education where and when I could.'

'Tom got 10 O-levels with no great effort. But by the time he'd got his A-levels, he had decided he'd had enough of school. I wanted him to go on to university, of course. I tried to talk him into seeing the sense of it, but he just refused. Now that's very hurtful; having your advice ignored and discounted by someone who used to set store by it.

'My wife says I clash with Tom because we are alike. We got on well when he was younger. The first disagreement was when he rejected the church. We're a church-going family and I found it impossible to accept that he wanted nothing to do with it. Ironically I'd cut myself off from religion in my teens for a while because I felt it was making too many demands on me, but I can't come to terms with my son rebelling in the same way.

'Tom is unemployed now. He had a good job. He lost it for misappropriating £80. I've surprised myself by being able to talk about it. Maybe I'm looking for sympathy. I do feel the need to discuss it, though the person I most want to talk it over with, Tom, doesn't want to know.

'Initially, when the money went missing, he was suspended. My wife heard first and she told me so I was prepared when he broke the news himself. I told him he'd been a fool and that he should have asked me for the money, whatever he needed it for. He insisted he'd only borrowed it and planned to return it before it was noticed. I thought I'd handled the situation calmly and quite well. But afterwards he said that I'd exploded and then preached at him in a self-righteous fashion.

'Being realistic, it was the most stupid thing for a bright lad to do – he had to be caught. I wonder if, at some unconscious level, he wanted to be caught. It was one way out of a humdrum job, perhaps the only way he could think of. On the other hand maybe he did need the money – he was about to go on holiday – and couldn't ask me because I'm dead set against borrowing and he knows it.

'There was a little run-in this week. I get a bit annoyed to see him just dossing around as if he hadn't a care in the world and I asked him what he was going to do now he hadn't a job. He got very arrogant and dismissive and shrugged his shoulders and I felt myself starting to boil. But I forced myself to stop and really think about what I wanted to say to him instead of letting the anger take over. Then I said; "Look, I don't approve of what you did, but whatever you do, I'll always love you." Tom got a bit choked, and so did I.

'After he'd left, I felt I still hadn't got it right. It hadn't been enough. I'd wanted to put my arms round him and hug him, but you can't do that to a grown man who's bigger than you, even if he is your son. I just wish there was some way to break down the barrier.

'There is another worry. It's to do with girls. Simon has got a steady girlfriend, who is a good steadying influence on him. I don't ask questions, but I was trying to tidy up the mess in his room recently and I came across a packet of Durex. It didn't bother me. I just thanked God he's responsible.

'But it did bring into focus the niggling fear at the back of my mind that where women are concerned, Tom is not quite normal. He's not interested in girls, never has been. There is just this one, close male friend he spends all this time with.

'I've no logical reason to think there is any more than that to it, but the situation gives me an uneasy feeling. Then I think "Well, what would it matter if he was gay, anyway?'' But I know I would find it very, very hard to accept. I'd take it personally. I'd feel there was something wrong with me.

'Let's be honest. Whoever you are, there are times when you must find your teenagers difficult; times when you inwardly come close to detesting them. But you never stop worrying about them. Their lack of activity drives me mad, the way they can sit around for hours on end without any apparent feelings of boredom or guilt.

'I have worked every day of my life since I left school. You'd think the least they could do is help in the house and keep their bedrooms tidy, without having to be nagged continually. It's become a bit corny to say National Service was a good thing, but you went in a boy and you came out a man. It took you away from the watchful eye of your parents when you were in your late teens, and gave them a break from the hassle, while you learned independence and how to look after yourself. There are less successful finishing schools.'

Alison, wife of a Church Minister, mother of Damien (18), Barry (16) and 14-year-old Rowena, all adopted:
'I'll be honest. We have two thoroughly rebellious teenagers, and our daughter hasn't got into her stride yet. I look around at the perfectly behaved teenagers of friends, academic-achievers who never step out of line, and I wonder if we've gone wrong somewhere. Or are those other apparently biddable young people simmering volcanoes underneath?

'You never actually know what happens behind other peoples' doors, do you? People are ashamed to tell you if their children are awful because it reflects on them. I don't know whether we have been very liberal or very strict parents. I've no yardstick to measure by.

'We wanted the children to grow into individuals with minds of their own, who would challenge authority and think for themselves. They certainly do that. I just didn't anticipate how hard it would make them to live with. But, then, five adults fighting for space in one house are bound to create tension. They take up so much space and create so much noise. You long for the time when you could put them to bed at seven and kiss them goodnight and settle down to a peaceful evening.

'They are very different, our three. Whether that is because they are not related genetically or because of their position in the family or what, I'll never know. Certainly Barry, the middle-child, the traditional difficult child in a family, is the biggest problem.

'He's just had two horrendous years at school, with disastrous exam results. He refused to re-take them, so he's at home all day with no work, no prospects. It's a degrading experience. His friends have done well. He's full of shame, though on the surface it's all covered up by scorn for "the pieces of paper" that say you are formally educated. Why should he go along with the rules of a society that is unjust and corrupt? Why should he jump through the hoops?, he says. The irony is that his ideas came from us. It's just that, in him, they are violent passions, uncontrolled.

'He has always had these violent enthusiasms, now they are accentuated by adolescence. He is totally committed to CND, goes on all the rallies and marches, hitch-hiking and sleeping out. I felt this was one of the reasons his school work was suffering so I have tried to get him to give some of them a miss. It has been the cause of some rows. His rages are terrible. He hits out, smashes things. He is completely out of control. Sometimes I wonder if I've got a psychotic person on my hands.

The other side of the coin is that Barry can be talkative and sociable. He's much loved by his friends and by their parents, who thinks he's a real live wire. When I think back he's exactly what he was as a young child: full of energy, loves being the centre of attention, inclined to show off, thinks he's no end of a macho fellow.

'When we've had a particularly bad spell, and I'm looking worn, friends will say, "We'll talk to him. We'll tell him what he's doing to you." I won't let them. What's the point? He knows what he's doing. He cries about it, we both do. He knows he is behaving badly. He just doesn't know what to do about it.

'Nor is it helped by the fact that his brother and sister think his behaviour is appalling and make no bones about it. They both think I spend far too much time pandering to Barry's tantrums.

'Rowena is a very stable person. She's self-conscious about her looks and absorbed in herself as young girls are, of course. She's also a budding feminist. Damien is a strong-willed boy with a strong moral conscience. He's never been academically-inclined, but he's good with his hands. He's got a job, a nice girl-friend, so I suppose I have little cause for complaint with Damien.

'The problems are more in the eyes of other people. He has lovely hair, which he wears very long, sometimes tied back. He rides a motor-bike and he mixes with motor-bike people. I know he has smoked pot. He was growing a strange plant in his room, which he assured me was a sunflower. I looked it up in a book and found it was cannabis. I asked him to remove it and he did.

'People are taken aback by his appearance. They say, "Why don't you make him cut his hair? I wouldn't have a son of mine with hair like that. I'd cut it off when he was asleep." I'm quite shocked by that. What right do I have to try and force him into a mould of my making? How do you set about making a man of 18 cut his hair? He will, he says, cut it when he's ready.

'We're moving away from this town soon and naturally we wanted the whole family to stay together. Damien refused. He said "Look Mum, I love you and Dad dearly, but my friends are a more important part of my life. I'm going to stay near them." It hurt, but I appreciated the honesty and he is right. Friends *are* more important to teenagers than family. Parents are people who are just there when they are needed.'

Christine, mother of 20-year-old Andrew and 17-year-old twins Peter and Susan:
'You daren't ask a question or make a remark without being accused of nagging. I only have to suggest to Peter that he might like a clean shirt when he is getting ready for a job interview, to have him stamp out of the room in a huff.

'A while back Andrew started a new job and I asked him if he was happy in it. He said, "I've got a job, haven't I? You're never satisfied." Honestly, they are so self-centred, so defensive, looking all the time for reasons for a row. It's always them and us.

'I suppose, to be fair, Andrew is proof that they grow out of it. Not long ago he would not walk down the street with me or sit in the same room with his father and me. Now if he sees me coming out of the supermarket he'll carry the shopping home for me and he'll occasionally even watch television with us!

'Peter is the worry. He was taken on a computer course and we were delighted, but he dropped out. "I only did it because you wanted me to," he said. So now he is unemployed. He goes out every night on his motor-bike, stays in bed half the day and borrows money from me for cigarettes, when I hate smoking. All I can do is sit tight and wait for him to grow up. He is very immature. I know he is trying to find himself, but it is hard on the rest of us while he searches.

'Susan on the other hand is a sensible girl, going well in the sixth form. I trust her completely. She talks to me about everything. She doesn't want a steady boy-friend yet – she wants to have a career. Nor is she interested in sleeping around. At school she says there are girls who do and girls who don't. Susan prefers to belong to the second group. Having brothers has been a help. She's seen them beating their heads against brick walls and decided it's not worth it. It's also given her a more realistic attitude towards boys. She can be friends with them without getting starry-eyed.'

Alan, works with handicapped children, married to Janet, has four children, the oldest 18:

'I'm looking forward to my children leaving home and I make no secret of it. I can't understand these fears people have about "the Empty Nest". If mine showed no interest, I'd be inclined to give them a push! I'm a great believer in the young setting out to build their own nest, and their own life, as soon as they can fly!

'I wouldn't recommend anyone, unless they are absolutely besotted with kids, having more than two. I'd also suggest you should have them while you are pretty young. By the time you get to your mid-forties and you have four kids old enough to make demands and let you know their forceful views, you feel as if you've never lived a life of your own. You get quite desperate for a chance to live just for yourself, to do your own thing.

'My wife is absolutely worn out. Partly it's her own fault. She has got into the habit of waiting on them. Now they are capable of looking after themselves to a lesser or greater extent, she is still at their beck and call. As long as she continues to wait on them, they continue to expect it.

'Mind you, I think we are all brain-washed into accepting anything an adolescent does as just part of a phase, when there can be a real medical reason occasionally. Take our eldest. He was always a difficult, over-active boy, but by the time he was in his mid-teens he was having outbursts of violence where he would hit everything in sight. Not people, fortunately, but he would smash anything breakable, hit the bonnet of a car hard enough to dent it.

'The slightest frustration of his wishes or denial of his demands could cause one of these tantrums. For a long time we told ourselves it was just adolescence, just part of growing up. Then we began to realise that the outbursts were happening at regular intervals, about every month. You could almost see the anger building up in him over a length of time, till it would just take one small disagreement to trigger the explosion.

'Because of my work, I have contact with doctors who are experts in mental health, and I had a chat to one of these about Robert's behaviour. He asked to see the lad. He gave him an EEG, and it turns out that my son has a physical condition of the brain, which causes these fits of over-activity.

'He is on pills now, and will have to be for the rest of his life. He is a changed person – reasonable, normal. Occasionally you see him start to get edgy and if you check, you'll find he's forgotten to take his pills. He's even good-humoured about being reminded regularly – just the sort of thing that would have caused an explosion a couple of years ago.

'The motto is that adolescence can mask other conditions, and we are far too ready to tolerate behaviour that would worry us out of our minds at any other time in a child or adult's life. I often wonder what might have happened eventually during one of Robert's outbreaks if he hadn't found a way of controlling it.

'He's a nice, ordinary kid now – almost ready to boot out of the nest, with the others hot on his heels! Seriously though, I'm looking forward to the time when my wife and I can be a couple again, enjoying each other's company and pursuing our interests. I think I'll probably enjoy being a grandfather more than being a Dad!'

Maureen, mother of three sons aged between 15 and 19:
'Darren, the 17-year-old, he drives me mad. He's so bloody dirty, you see. It's disgusting. You can't get him to have a bath. When he washes, it's a case of wiping a cloth round his neck, leaving a trail in the grime.

'I'm always losing my temper with him. "For heaven's sake, you stink," I shout at him. He shouts back, "Can't you stop nagging for a minute. Leave me alone. I'm tired. I've been at work all day."

'What does he think the rest of us have been doing all day? His Dad does a hard day's work on a milk round, and Darren never lifts a finger to help him in the garden. Or to help me around the house for that matter. He's lucky to have a job these days, even a factory job.

'To be fair, he enjoys the job. At least he enjoys the beer money it brings in. That's another thing, the drinking. He's out drinking in some of the toughest clubs in town nearly every night. I worry about him. He's well over 6 feet tall and very tough-looking. He's a walking invitation to other lads to pick fights to cut him down to size.

'He gets upset when I go on at him sometimes. The other day he said to me, "I don't know why you ever had me. You didn't want me." That made me *mad* – all those years of caring and that's the way he sees it. Maybe I'm making a mountain out of a molehill. People tell me to ignore the dirty neck and his mucky habits. Someone told me it's a way of getting attention and he's doing it deliberately.

'Others say he'll change when he gets a girl. Well, he's had girls. They've got tired of him too. He doesn't care. He prefers drinking himself into a stupor with his mates. His older brother is marvellous: smart, good-looking, a good worker. He goes out too, he takes a drink, but he knows not to overdo it.

'The youngest is a lot younger, so he's always had to have a lot more attention. I sometimes think that maybe Darren feels left out between the two of them. But then I think why should he? I've never shown favouritism. I've treated them all equally. Maybe he's just a lazy sod.'

Sheila, social worker, mother of Jane (17) and Stephen (20):
'What does Jane do that bothers us? What doesn't she do? She's everything we ever feared our daughter would turn into. It hasn't always been so. I can date the change in her from the time she turned 14 and found a new set of friends.

'Her old friends were smashing kids. This crowd are totally anti-parent and she's picked up their attitudes. If a parent says it or thinks it, it has to be wrong. They can be scornful and unpleasant. I listen to Jane talking on the phone and can't believe it's my daughter.

'Because Joe and I are social workers, people assume we are experts. "What did I do wrong?" they ask, when their kids start kicking over the traces. I don't believe it's anything you've done or failed to do. After a certain age, other influences are stronger than yours. You have to pray that you made a big enough impression when they were listening.

'Another thing, everyone is an individual. Stephen was even-tempered and placid even as a baby. He floated through adolescence in the same placid fashion. Jane has been volatile and temperamental from the year dot.

'She refuses to use her potential and as a result she did badly in her exams and is out of work. She's full of scorn for her brother who is at college "conforming". I'm sure she envies him secretly.

'When she was a bit younger the big bone of contention was going out and what time to come home. We got the usual – '*Everyone can do it except me.*' When you meet the other parents you find out it isn't true at all. They play parents off against each other.

'I'm sure there's an element of pleasure in our disapproval. Like putting on bright-blue nail-varnish and holding it under my nose to ask if I like it, when she knows I loathe it. It's the same with the current boy-friend. He's a biker, pushing 30, divorced and clad from head to toe in black leather. When he turned up at the door I bit back my horror and invited him in for a cup of tea and a chat. I'm sure Jane wanted us to rant and rave about his unsuitability; then she could convince herself he was really the man for her.

'I don't approve of her friends or her way of life and I see no reason in general why I should pretend. But I accept it. I'd accept anything that would make her happy, but she is so unhappy it's heartbreaking. She doesn't know what she wants or who she is and I suspect she feels a failure.

'I know that most people go through adolescence and come out at the other end normal, reasonably happy adults. If every kid who went off the rails in their teens stayed off, our prisons would be even fuller. There's light at the end of the tunnel, but the ride through it is fairly rocky for us.'

Dennis, a self-employed shop-fitter. He has three daughters, the youngest handicapped:
'Hardly a day passes without the subject of Karen coming up in our house: what went wrong with her, what did we do wrong? We've accepted that nothing we can do will change her, but I know June, my wife, still feels we're somehow responsible. But look at Bernice, our second daughter, who is smashing. If we were such lousy parents, surely it would have rubbed off on her too?

'No, they are just different people, always have been, even in looks. Karen is big and strongly built, Bernice is dainty and feminine. Karen's problems began at school. She started walking out of the grounds at lunch-time and not coming back in the afternoon. They assigned a teacher to watch her; I had a few sharp words with her and the phase seemed to pass.

'I suppose I missed a lot of the day-to-day hassle of bringing up the girls, because I was a salesman and away a lot. As a couple we had one rule. We always stuck together and backed each other up in a disagreement. There was never the chance to ask Mum because she's the softer touch or get round Dad, when Mum has already said no.

'When she left school, Karen went to work as an au-pair with a family near Geneva. It seemed a good idea for an energetic, adventurous girl. Before she'd served half her one-year contract, I got a garbled phone-call from her employer asking for the money to pay her fare home. They didn't want her looking after their kids any longer.

'It seemed she'd been bringing young men home to spend the night with her. Karen's story was that they were soldiers with nowhere to sleep and that nothing happened. Well, I'm not naïve – I've been a soldier too!

'We sent the fare and went to meet her at the airport, but she never turned up. We contacted the police, but they didn't seem bothered. Three weeks later we got a pitiful phone-call from a hospital. She'd had an abortion and there had been complications. I wasn't even angry any more, just very sad to have my daughter turn out like that.

'We thought she'd learned her lesson. She came home, enrolled at a local college – and immediately got in on the drug scene. Before long she was spending all her evenings at a pub that is notorious for drugs and under-age drinking. I found her there one night, with a rather well-off girl-friend. I demanded she come home with me but she refused.

'I was mad. I drove to the girl-friend's posh house and told her father where his daughter was. Apparently he went straight round and dragged her out, literally, by the hair, in front of all her friends.

'Karen didn't come home till a couple of nights later. I can still see her now, standing at the top of the stairs, dead arrogant, calling down to me. "If you don't keep your nose out of other people's business, you're going to get duffed up," she said.

'I'd never smacked the girls from the time they were about 10 or 11, when they became what I'd call young ladies. But I lost my temper. I hit her, hard enough to make her cry. I told her to pack her case and get out.

'I'm glad to say she didn't. She just cried and slunk away. It's odd, but after that we got nearer to being friends than we had ever managed. I think she respected me a bit more. It was treatment she understood.

'I'm not proud of hitting a girl. If I'd done it to Bernice, she would never have spoken to me again. But then she never needed it. Bernice has never put a foot wrong.

'I'd like to be able to say that Karen grew out of her bad ways. But she hasn't. She's been in and out of hospital for drug addiction and she's currently living with an addict. June and I have had to come to terms with the fact that she is not the daughter we would have chosen, but she is our flesh and blood and we'll stick by her, whatever.

'But why did it happen? Any problems from having a handicapped sister that Karen had to live with, Bernice encountered too. Both of them were given an equal amount of love and attention. What is it that makes two little girls take a completely different path from adolescence onwards? I wish I could answer that.'

OVER THE WORST: the liberal, the light-hearted and the survivors. Some lucky parents float painlessly through their children's adolescent years, wondering what all the fuss is about. Others, learning by experience, find a sense of humour, a sense of perspective and a formula that might horrify the family next door but works for them. Most survive!

Paula, mother of three sons and a daughter, the oldest in his early twenties, the youngest 12:
'As long as they aren't mugging old ladies, sticking needles in their

arms or getting drunk regularly, I don't complain. The two older boys have often brought their girl-friends back to stay the night. Having sussed out beforehand that they are sleeping together, I fix them up with two mattresses in the front room. It doesn't cause me any embarrassment. I would find it much harder to be hypocritical and make a point of putting them in separate rooms.

'When I was a teenager, romancing was done on the doorstep or in the entry and kept secret from your parents. I would hate to put my kids in that sort of situation. Secrecy tends to blow up the sexual part of a relationship out of all proportion. I want them to be aware it is perfectly normal and only a part of a relationship.

'I think the secret of getting on well with adolescents is putting in a lot of spadework then they are young. I always told mine that I was inclined to be neurotic and worry about them because I loved them. As a result – probably because they feel sorry for me – they never stay out late without telling me where they are going or ringing me.

'The only shock we've had was when Paul, the eldest, was in his first term at university. He announced that he was leaving to tour with a rock group he'd joined. We were horrified, but we have always encouraged them to do what they want with their lives.

'This was the point at which it was put to the test. We held our breath while he spent the summer holiday with the group. Just before the new term began, he said he was bored and wanted to go back to university. What a relief. There had been no showdown – it was his decision. On the whole it seems silly to make a fuss over a few years in everyone's life. It's just a stage. It will pass.'

John, a teacher, father of two daughters in their late teens, Helen and Jane, and 14-year-old David:
'We don't approve of everything they do, but we are very pleased and grateful that they tell us about it. Our whole family relationship is built on trust and honesty and an easy repartee.

'Our children can say anything to us and so can their friends. We had 22 young people staying overnight once and they told my wife Elizabeth and I that we were more like students ourselves than parents. I'm still trying to work out if that is a compliment!

'I think some of our friends think we're soft with our lot, but then I know that some of the boys and girls with very strict parents are telling one story at home and doing something quite different outside.

'We don't lay down rules. Elizabeth and I go to church but we don't force the children to come. Nevertheless they come. What I ask from them is that they see other people's points of view. What I hate is arrogance in teenagers. My son will sometimes say, "That's rubbish, you don't know what you're talking about" and then I have to cut him down to size. I can take it but I'd hate to think of him saying it to another adult.

'The older girl, Helen, and I are very close. We share a lot of confidences and a lot of opinions. As far as relationships go, we've always told them that nobody wants second-hand goods. When Helen broke off with her boy-friend of several years she said, "I'm very glad I didn't start a sexual relationship with him."

'Jane is a complicated mixture – so outspoken that people some-times take her as abusive, but incredibly generous and loving too. Unfortunately some people only see the first side.

'She recently got involved in an episode that caused her mother and me a lot of distress. She and a few others went joy-riding in a borrowed car. There was an accident, eventually a court case – a terrible time. We've always drummed honesty into Jane and of course she told the police every last detail, incriminating herself far more than she needed to or than the others did.

'It's over now, but we are going away for the weekend and she has asked if she can hold a party at the house in our absence. She is very indignant. She said "I told you everything. I was completely honest, and now you don't trust me." Well, I *want* to trust her again, but . . .'

Julie, a secretary, mother of Adrian, Debbie and Stephen:
'For a few years we were often like strangers sharing a house, but now there are times when we are a real family together and it's lovely. Those times get more frequent as the children get older.

'I feel we're over the worst of it, like the time when Adrian came home and said, "I've left school". We had no idea he'd been planning it, but what could we do? He was over 16. It's painful to see them making mistakes that will affect the rest of their lives. It hurts that they are no longer under your control. You can only guide them – and so diplomatically they don't know what you are doing. Otherwise there will be a confrontation.

'Having adolescents around has certainly taught me diplomacy. I learned early that they won't tell you anything if you ask directly. You get more information out of them about their feelings and their plans by asking about a friend. "What is Jim doing these days? Thinking of studying accountacy is he? What do you think of that as a career?" You will hear an awful lot of boring stuff, but there's a good chance you'll also hear what they are thinking.

'Girls seem to keep their common-sense and awareness of other people's feelings better throughout adolescence. Debbie, though we had lower expectations of her than the boys, is at college now with good job prospects. The two boys both gave up working at about the age of 13. There was no replacement activity, just idleness. The older one in particular was terribly unhappy because he was so aware of the disapproval coming from all sides.

'Debbie comes and goes as she pleases. Well, she's 19 now. From her mid-teens it was more a case of her telling us what time she would be home than us telling her when to come in. She trained us to it.

'I think you have to lower your standards, accept a different set of standards from those you were brought up on. I was aware one of my sons was having a sexual relationship with his steady girl-friend, but when the girl found out I knew she was distraught. What would I think of her? I found myself in the strange position of having to comfort her and assure her it was all right. I make the distinction between a steady relationship and promiscuity.'

June, mother of Kelly, 19 and now married, 18-year-old twins Cathy and Terri and a 14-year-old son:
'When she was 13½, Cathy started going out with a 19-year-old boy. A nice boy, but at that age I figured he wasn't going to be satisfied with just sharing a cup of coffee. I've always talked openly to my girls and I said to her, "Are you and Peter wanting a sexual relationship, because if so you must think about contraception". She said, "No, Mum, he's willing to wait". When she was 14 she decided to go on the pill. I went with her to the doctor's. The only thing he queried was whether it was a steady relationship. She and Peter are still together now.

'At the time, both alternatives worried me a bit. Putting a 14-year-old on the pill or risking a 15-year-old mother. Now I'm absolutely confident I made the right decision. I was 23 when I got married and I hadn't been to bed with my husband. But things change. I try to keep an open mind. I listen to the girls talking. I read their magazines to keep up-to-date. Because my husband is away a lot, I've often been both mother and father. I'm used to making decisions.

'The other two girls went on the pill at around 16/17 when they had steady boy-friends. They told me and I thought they were very sensible and responsible. All three were very mature girls. My son is much younger for his age, about two years behind the girls at that age.

'Only two things they have done really upset me. One is lying – I hate them not to tell me the truth when I am open with them. The other is stealing. Just before Christmas four years ago, I got a phone call from the police station. The twins and a friend had been caught shoplifting – goods to the value of £80, all presents for the family and friends.

'I was flaming mad. When I got to take them home, I thumped them and swore at them and promised them that, thanks to their antics, we would have the saddest Christmas of their lives. I kept to the promise. There were no presents for anyone, no special food. It was the saddest, quietest Christmas possible and we all suffered, but it certainly taught the twins a lesson.

'All the girls are stable young adults now. We have a good relationship. I think too many people make the mistake of not listening to their adolescents, not praising them when they deserve it and most of all, not treating them as individuals with minds of their own.'

Bernard, psychiatrist, father of two sons:
'Your professional training goes out the window when your own family is involved. You are just another confused father, wondering where you went wrong. There's a joke in our house that I used the works of Freud in bringing up my children – I hit them with them when things got too much!

'The older boy was mature, serious, worked hard at school – the sort of boy who almost worries you because he is so free of teenage problems! So much so, that when his younger brother began to turn into a prickly, typically teenage character, it was as if John was with us, seeing it from our viewpoint not his brother's. There were, in effect, three adults in the house, trying to understand and cope with this adolescent.

'What happened was that at around 13/14, Matthew developed a thing about going to school. Call it a phobia if you like. We took it at face value at first. When he said he was ill, we let him stay home and dutifully sent off a letter to school. Then it became obvious that his ailments were cropping up on the same days and we began to question him.

'He wouldn't tell us why he didn't want to go. He wouldn't talk about it. There were refusals, tantrums, tears. He was desperately keen that I shouldn't go up to the school which he saw as a further humiliation. We didn't make a big issue of it, but by talking to staff on parents' evening, it became obvious that it was games he was trying to avoid.

'It was an all-boys school, very keen on sports. He is no good at games, hates them all, which has always been hard for me to take because I'm an enthusiast. Added to that, he was at the time very slight and thin, and he came in for a bit of teasing when he had to take his clothes off. At that age, to be made fun of can be the end of the world.

'I remember having a talk with him, all very oblique, a lot left unsaid, but making it clear that he was going to have to cope with it. I suppose I played a lot on his feelings for his mother, how much worry he was causing her. After that he made the effort and there was no more school-refusal.

'Gradually the academic and other aspects of school became more important, and he found his niche. He found what he was good at, he got his confidence back. He involved himself heavily in voluntary work and gave up physical activities as far as he could. Matthew is at university now, though we did fear he wouldn't get in at one stage. Though he is probably academically more able than his brother, he is totally uncompetitive. He just cannot see the point of doing more work than is absolutely necessary!

'If John, the older one, has a problem it is his shyness. He's at University too. He came home one weekend and there was obviously something on his mind though we didn't pry. When we were out, he left a letter addressed to his mother, but with instructions that she could show it to me. The gist of it was that he'd fallen for a girl who didn't reciprocate his feelings. It was making him miserable and he didn't know what to do about the situation.

'On the one hand I found it touching that he should turn to us for help. On the other, maybe it showed a degree of dependence that wasn't healthy. I don't know. We wrote him an Agony Aunt reply and that was the end of it. He didn't discuss the outcome.

'To be truthful, I know very little of what my sons are thinking or doing. You don't expect to be told at their ages. They talk far more to my wife. They have always had an easier relationship with her, probably because she takes things more calmly.

'I'm inclined to get anxious. They make a joke of it now. John will come in and say: "Dad, I've got something to tell you – Is your heart rate going up?"'

Anne, Deputy Warden at a community centre, mother of a son and two daughters, aged from 13 to 20:
'I keep waiting for the problems, but they just haven't happened. I'm enjoying having teenagers. They are marvellous companions and we are still very close as a family. When I suggested that the girls might like to go somewhere with their friends this year instead of coming away with us on holiday, there was general indignation. They do their own things, but the thought of no family holiday horrifies them.

'Maybe we get on so well because we have a lot in common. They are all mathematicians except me. My husband is head of a maths department and our eldest daughter is studying maths at Cambridge. We are all interested and involved in outdoor activities. Another point is that my husband is very sweet-tempered. He hates pop music, but he will never complain. He will simply not go into the room where it is playing.

'I've always talked to them about everything – politics, religion, sex. I've told the girls about contraception though I do not believe in sleeping around. I must admit I would have been surprised, knowing them, if one of them had asked to go on the pill at an early age.

'Both had their own clothes allowance at sixteen and they haven't looked too bad. Some of their friends look quite extraordinary. They have been made to save for anything they wanted. Both had a spell of going to discos and quickly grew out of it.

'If you get it right in the pre-school years, I'm sure it will be easier during adolescence. You have to learn to be friends with your children early and start letting go of them as soon as it is safe. Tony, our son, started going to school on his own when he was six. It's just a gradual process from there and adolescence is the final stage.'

SINGLE PARENTS

Is it harder bringing up teenagers single-handed? Yes – and surprisingly, no! It's easier for one strong-minded woman 'because I can make the decisions on where they go and how they behave without having to argue the case with a husband who probably has different ideas'.

It's harder for another, still deeply hurt emotionally (if not physically) following a heated argument with her 15-year-old son. 'He hit me. We were arguing over what time he should come in and he punched me on the arm. I just sat down and cried. Afterwards he tried to pretend he'd been playing, but I know anger when I see it. I doubt he'd have lost control so easily if he had a father here to back me up.'

Harder too, for 35-year-old divorcee Susan, mother of 14-year-old Donna. 'I'm not a saint, but I have to behave like one to set my daughter a good example. No live-in boy-friends and painting the town red for me. How can I ask her to be sensible and moral unless I am myself?'

Always there are financial constraints. Often there is long-distance antagonism between the parent who has custody and the absent one, with the teenager torn between the two. Many parents felt their teenagers coped well with having only one parent, but had suffered badly from living through a bitter divorce or separation. Others took this theory with a pinch of salt, like Liz:

'I used to say my two were awful because of the nastiness of the divorce and me having to cope alone. But since I've been back at work and heard stories from other parents of teenagers, I'm inclined to think it doesn't make a blind bit of difference what your home set-up is. Most teenagers are a bit of a pain. Single parenthood is just a useful excuse to blame it on.'

Marjorie, mother of David (18) and Russell (16). Both boys attended independent boarding schools:
'Russell is the problem. He is reserved, unsure of himself and hard to talk to. I can see a lot of myself in him, which at least helps me to understand him. I think he resents his older brother being more socially at ease and doing better at school.

'Last year he was particularly moody and depressive. I know that is part of growing up, but Russell's secretiveness, the total lack of communication between us, did cause me a lot of distress. We never argue, but then we never communicate either.

'Last year, I was worried about what he was doing, about the people he was mixing with. I got over that to some extent by persuading him to bring his friends home. He's always been reluctant to do that. I invited one girl myself, when she phoned up. She seemed amazed, and Russell went to great lengths explaining to me that the girl was rather way-out in her appearance. I said not to worry, she probably wouldn't think much of the way I dressed either. It apparently all boiled down to him thinking I would be shocked by his friends and criticise them. Neither of my boys can take criticism.

'There was one particularly bad incident last year, where Russell was suspected of being involved in an indecent assault case. It was a mistake and he was innocent. My older son said all along it was. "Russell may be silly in some ways, but he knows how to behave," he said.

'Though one part of me knew David was right, I was desperately worried. In a way it was a turning point between Russell and me. For the first time he saw me as a person, not only his mother. I was no longer someone who was there just to take what life handed out. He saw me angry, distressed and beside myself with worry: a vulnerable human being in fact, something adolescents don't recognise in their parents. It forced him to look outside himself and brought us closer together.'

'In the past year he has improved. He has good days as well as bad now. He is knuckling down to work for his O-levels. If you get him in the right situation, at the right moment, he may even discuss something with you. Television is very useful in this way. If I can get him to watch a programme, perhaps about some aspect of relationships, I find he'll often be prepared to chat about it afterwards and give me his opinions on the subject.

'As far as girls go, I wouldn't dream of prying into their lives. It's none of my business what my older son and his girl-friend do. It was a great relief to me that there were male staff at their schools, who could talk to them about those subjects. It's one of the areas that is difficult for a mother bringing up sons alone.

'When I came across a girlie-magazine in Russell's room it did give me a jolt, but I didn't let it show. He'd hidden it, so I fished it out, took it downstairs and flicked through it in front of him. "If you like these, there's no need to hide them," I said. "I don't mind." I don't think he knew what to say. He'd obviously expected me to be shocked. He still hides them though.

'I suffered a nervous breakdown a year ago. The counselling I've had has been aimed at teaching me to think more of myself and less of my sons. One of the problems with being a single parent is that you get too involved with your children. They are, after all, the only things in your life. You put them before everyone, including yourself.

'I'm learning to see them as adults instead of my children. They may drink or smoke and do various other things I don't approve of, but I cannot stop them. As long as they are conscious of my concern for their safety and let me know where and how they are – that's all I have the right to expect at their age. It's a hard lesson – but I'm learning.'

Karen, divorced. She has a daughter (18), and son (14) who live with her:
'It was easier with my daughter. Whether that was because her father was with us then or just that she is a girl I don't know. I understood her better. I could remember doing the things she did. I took the line of least resistance on matters which, in the long run are not that important. So, when she wanted to wear make-up at 12 or 13, instead of saying you're too young, I helped her to do it properly. Better to have her looking nice than have her slipping outside with a scrubbed face and putting it on messily down the road out of my sight. I know what it's like to be a young girl.

'She has had plenty of boy-friends and though I had no reason to think she was sleeping with them, I used to hold my breath, waiting, worrying that she might get pregnant.

'Each birthday, I'd think, "Well that's another year over and at least she's not pregnant!'' Now I relax. She is old enough to take responsibility for her own life. Mostly she has been a nice pleasant girl, easy to be with. Except for a bad spell, just before she reached her teens, when she turned briefly into a totally disagreeable human being, sullen and aggressive. I breathed another sigh of relief when I realised that was only a short stage and quickly passed.

'My son is different. He seems much less mature for a start. Most of his free time seems to be spent riding around on his bike. I hear he meets girls on these rides, but he hasn't told me.

'He can be very aggressive, argumentative and rude. Particularly when he has been to visit his father. It takes him some to settle down again. You can't tell him what to do. His attitude is that he is the man in the house, very macho. It is hard not to react with aggression yourself and to remember that he has been through a lot of moves and upheavals and probably feels torn in loyalty between me and his father. On the other hand, am I making this an excuse for all his behaviour? You see he doesn't tell me what he is thinking or feeling and I can't get inside his head.'

Patricia, mother of four children, ranging from 22 to 5. She's divorced; a second long-standing relationship has ended, and she now lives with her 16-year-old daughter and 5-year-old son:
'I've disowned Cheryl, my 19-year-old. She's living round the corner with her boy-friend, but we don't speak. I've had enough of her total selfishness and her unreasonable behaviour. You don't go on putting up forever with someone who makes your life unbearable just because she happens to be your child. Why should you? As far as I'm concerned, she is now just another adult I do not get on with. That's the end of it.

'She was okay as a kid – they all are till they decide they want independence and your rules don't suit. As soon as she was at work, giving me a couple of pounds a week, well she thought she'd bought the right to do exactly as she pleased.

'I remember once when she was seventeen, telling her to be in by a certain time at night. Her arrogant answer was, "What will you do if I'm not?" I told her I'd lock her out – and when she didn't get back till the early hours, I did just that. She smashed a window with her crash helmet and got in that way. She doesn't want to talk about the differences, our Cheryl, never has. She sees things her way. Nothing you can say will change it.

'The final straw was when I took a lodger, a young lad, to help make ends meet. I explained to the girls that we'd have to share rooms for a while. Well the girls don't get on with each other at all, so because it is the biggest, I told Cheryl I'd have to share hers. She went mad and refused, but I ignored her and moved in. The first night after moving in, I went out for the evening. When I got home, she had the bedroom barricaded.

'I couldn't do anything with her. I had to call her Dad who got into the room and tried to reason with her. His attitude didn't suit either. She went for him with a pair of scissors and he ended up hitting her. We had the police in in the end – that's when she moved out.

'I won't say that deep down it doesn't hurt to cut your daughter out of your life. But I'm a tough lady, I've had to be, bringing up my kids alone. I run my own second-hand business. I make my own decisions.

'Would it have been different if she'd had two parents? Not at this stage. Anyway her father can't handle her either. After the big row, he started thinking along those lines. He said he'd made his mistakes years ago. If he'd been firmer with her as a child, she'd have been a different girl today. Would she? Your guess is as good as mine.

'My 16-year-old daughter can be very trying, too. She has no thought for anyone else either. In fact I'm not speaking to her at the moment, but I'm sure we'll get over it. The 22-year-old now – he's a lovely lad. Immature for his age I suppose, but very considerate. He doesn't live at home but he comes to see me regularly, two or three times a week. He went to live with his Gran when the marriage broke up. Maybe it was her influence or maybe it's just his character, but there was never any of this teenage performance with him.

'My boy-friend who lived with us, Cheryl got on well with him . . . She was the first to the hospital to see her baby brother when he was born. There wasn't any jealousy about him taking my attention. In fact the only contact we have now is when she rings up occasionally and asks to speak to little Ricky. I don't deny her that.

'I never expected total obedience and love from my daughter. I wouldn't claim to love my mother, but I wouldn't treat her like dirt. All you ask is to be taken into consideration occasionally. I suppose the mistake we all make is that we don't talk enough to each other. But how can you talk to someone who won't listen?'

Kay, a widow, bringing up her only daughter, Louise, single-handed. Louise is nearly 14, an attractive, mature girl. Kay works part-time in an office:
'It's been like losing a child. Maybe that sounds melodramatic, but watching my daughter grow away from me, has, at times, been something like a bereavement.

'My own fault I suppose. After my husband died, when Louise was only four, I put all my energy into her. I didn't try to make new friends – she became my best friend. I took her everywhere. Trips, holidays and outings were all geared to suit her.

'Not that Louise was isolated from children of her own age. She's always been a confident, popular girl who made friends easily. Often one or two of her friends would come along when Louise and I went out.

'I don't know what I thought was going to happen when she began to grow up. Maybe I hoped things would always stay the same – that my daughter would be the first one in the world to stay exactly as she was at 9 or 10 forever. I was totally unprepared for her wanting to go her own way, even though I could obviously see she was growing up physically. She started her periods before she was 12.

'Then, almost overnight, she changed. Whereas I'd always been able to buy her clothes for her without any clash of tastes, or guide her towards the most suitable things, suddenly if I liked something, she hated it. Her taste was awful to make matters worse. She liked cheap, tarty clothes from the boutiques, which though they fitted her looked years too old. And she demanded high heels, her ears pierced, and her hair cut short so that it stood up all round.

'Whether I tried to reason with her or to put my foot down firmly, the result was the same. I ended up shouting or crying, and she stormed out of the house, slamming the doors so they nearly came off the hinges.

'I'd always been able to reason with her and influence her, but I just began to believe she hated me. If I suggested going out somewhere together, this expression of scorn would spread across her face, or she'd say "I'd rather go with Julie". If I put my hand on her arm, say crossing the road, she'd shrug it off, as if I'd hit her. When she wasn't out, she was in her room alone, playing records. No amount of persuading could get her to come downstairs and sit with me. It was living with a stranger I couldn't get through to.

'I kept wondering if they all go through this. You don't like to talk too openly about it to relatives or neighbours – I suppose because you feel somehow to blame. Everybody *says* adolescents can be hard to live with, but surely they don't all reject their parents completely? And not this early? I thought at least I'd have my child for longer than 12 or 13 years.

'What alarms me most is that my own attitude seems to be hardening. I just can't go on caring. A few times, I've seen Louise and a couple of her friends hanging around with a crowd of boys who have a very bad reputation locally. Of course I've tried to warn her and reason with her, but to no avail. The next day she's with the same lads again.

'Lately I've found myself thinking, "Okay, let her get into trouble with the police. Let her get a reputation, let her get pregnant. That'll teach her a lesson. Then she'll have to come running to me for help.' Isn't that awful?

'You keep searching for little signs it might be getting better. The other day, after her tea, she was going out, and I felt too weary to go through the routine of asking where she was going and telling her what time to come home. She walked out the door, then she came back in again, and said "I've done my homework, I'm going round to Julie's, I'll be back around 8 – okay, Mum?" I couldn't believe it. It was the most sociable, sensitive thing she'd said in months!

'I've begun to wonder if, maybe, you have to distance yourself brutally – as Louise has done with me, and as I feel myself doing with her occasionally – before you can start to get back together again, as two adults.'

Delia, mother of a son and daughter, now 22 and 20, and a 16-year-old son. She works as a secretary. Two years ago, Delia discovered that her husband was having an affair with one of her friends. There were rows, recriminations, and he left home temporarily. They are now living together again in an unhappy truce, with their youngest son, John:

'However mature or blasé teenagers may act, don't let anyone convince you that the break-up of their parents' marriage has no effect on them. By 18, they are able to cope – they are pretty much leading their own lives by then – but at 14 or 16, it is still very painful for them.

'I didn't tell the children what was going on when I first found out about my husband's affair. In particular I wanted to keep it from John. Recently I found out that he knew from the start, but he never talked to anyone about it. The message he'd picked up from the silent tensions in the house was that these things should not be brought out into the open; you must keep your feelings bottled up.

'And that's exactly what he does now. On the surface he is a bright, happy, very physical and demonstrative boy. By which I mean that like a lot of boys that age, he has this uncontrollable energy. He's always hugging me or picking me up or playfully thumping me! But underneath he is frightened of so many things. He doesn't tell me, he says very little to me, but I know.

'The older boy, Richard, was about to leave home when the break-up came. He knew I didn't want him to go, that I was desperately lonely. But he went. Young people are selfish. Richard is a chauvinist. He has no respect for women and I think that stems from his attitude to me. He disapproved of the way I behaved, accepting his father back, not showing a great deal of pride. I think that has brushed off on his dealings with girl-friends.

'Rachel was very, very angry with her father. She wrote him a letter and he was shaken rigid by it. It was one of the few things about the whole affair which shook his confidence. She cried and cried. It was as if her whole world had collapsed. Yet she is the one who will, in the long run, be least affected by it. She is so balanced. She takes a very objective view of both me and her father.

'I don't think it's affected her attitude to marriage. Actually, I believe young people have a healthier attitude than my generation had. We did a lot of flirting and two-timing at their age. As far as I can see, with them everything is above-board and honest. They may go to bed together, which was less likely to happen in my circle, but everyone is quite open about it; nobody is having the wool pulled over their eyes.'

STEP PARENTS

Not all step-parents are wicked, even viewed through the hyper-critical eyes of their teenage step-children. I met boys and girls who spoke of step-parents with acceptance and affection. They did, however, tend to be older teenagers, or they were talking about the spouse of their absent parent, who they only met on visits and holidays.

However, there are undoubtedly many teenagers and many step-parents (or common-law step-parents, if such a title exists) for whom the relationship means war. Brenda Maddox in her book *Step-parenting* came to the conclusion that, 'Adolescence is probably the worst time for a child to become a step-child. The young look to the step-parent as a replacement for the lost parent; the older ones, with clearer memories of the real parent, reject the intruder.'

One of the big stumbling-blocks is authority. Teenagers are not too keen on taking orders from their own parents; they are doubly resentful of a newcomer waltzing in and taking over parental authority. Yet, to sit by and listen to what one step-father described as 'this arrogant little yob treating my wife like dirt' is often more than the new partner can stand.

Liz, a community worker at a centre for homeless and unemployed teenagers, says: 'One of the commonest causes of homelessness in the lads we see (far more boys than girls come here) is the arrival of the new step-father or Mum's live-in boy-friend. The new man seems to take an instant dislike to the boy and tries to impose his standards of behaviour on him. There are rows, sometimes physical violence. The boy leaves or is thrown out. Often, when you talk to them, you can't understand how the step-father can dislike the boy. Mostly, they are ordinary, likeable kids.

'I know it takes two to make an argument, but I do feel that the older man, with more experience of life should be the one to try and prevent it. It also seems that mothers, though they are often torn between the two and continue to see the son secretly, don't put up much of a stand in their kid's defence.'

Another painful possibility, familiar to anyone involved with teenagers' problems, is attraction between the step-child and the step-parent. Usually it is the new father (or Mum's boy-friend) taking an excessive interest in the pretty daughter; occasionally it's a young stepmother and son. It is the stuff of Greek tragedy.

More commonplace, for a teenager who has grown very close to the single parent, are feelings of jealousy and resentment at being replaced. At least that's how they will view it. Or the resentment may centre on the absent parent being replaced. There may be shock, embarrassment or even disgust at the idea of their parent embarking on a sexual relationship. It can be a bumpy ride for all parties.

Brenda Maddox feels that the biggest mistake step-parents make is in trying too hard to act the part of a parent, when quite a different role is called for. Certainly most of the teenagers I met who talked approvingly of their mother or father's new partner were describing not a replacement parent, but an understanding older friend.

Barbara, with her daughter Jenny, has lived through a series of emotional traumas that make the average spell of adolescent rebellion sound like a picnic. Barbara is a teacher, the mother of a 10-year-old daughter, and of Jenny, a hyper-slender 16-year-old, with watchful eyes. The household is completed by Andy, the girls' stepfather. Barbara no longer dreads the moment he walks in the door of their modern, semi-rural home and comes face to face with her elder daughter. She no longer waits for the explosion:

'Things are better now,' she says. 'Not perfect, but tolerable. Partly it is because Andy has learned to take several paces back and leave me to cope with Jenny; partly it's because she is growing up and finding a life of her own outside the triangle.'

The parental triangle is made up of Andy, Barbara and Barbara's ex-husband, Don. She left him, taking the two girls. 'If anyone in this day and age is to blame in a divorce situation, then he was the guilty party. For many reasons – not least that he was having an affair with a friend of mine.

'I kept a lot of the sordid side of it from the girls and in doing so, I now realise I lost out. Their father was not so scrupulous. It's a cliché to say children are used as pawns in divorce, but Jenny certainly was. She was bombarded with stories about my wickedness.

'To make matters worse, shortly after the divorce, he had a heart attack. I travelled long distances to take the children to his bed-side every day. When he began to feel better he turned to me and said: "You caused this." The girls heard. It had its effect on Jenny.

'When Andy first came to live with us, her father showed her a passage in the Bible which said that you would go to hell if you committed adultery. From then on, she firmly believed I was wicked. It was there in the Bible. Adolescents do sometimes turn to the Bible when they are under stress, in the same way they join religious cults.

'After we married, Jenny's behaviour towards Andy was – well, it was total war. She shut herself in her room and refused to be with us. When forced to go out as part of the family, she had to make it clear to everyone that Andy was not her father. I remember her in a shoe-shop, saying very loudly: "I wonder if my real father would like these shoes, Andy." Quite bizarre. She had to disassociate herself publicly from him.

'There were arguments over the usual teenage things, like staying out later, but when she became rude to me, Andy would fly to my defence, with "How dare you speak to your mother like that!" Of course that fuelled the fire.

'Meal times invariably ended with her screaming at him, "You bastard, I hate you." Twice he lost control and hit her. I think Andy was completely bewildered. He realised there would be difficulties, but he thought he could handle them. He hasn't been married before, so he has no experience of parenting. I think he believed his degree in psychology would help – but real life is not quite like case studies.

'For four years I've never had a day when I wasn't torn between my husband and my daughter. Two years ago I thought I couldn't take any more. During another mealtime argument, Jenny threw a glass of orange juice at Andy. It was just another incident, but to Andy it was the final straw. He said, "That's it, I'm leaving." I said, "No, you're not, Jenny is leaving."

'Over and over, she had told me that she hated living here and wanted to be with her father. People who knew the situation said I should let her go, but before that I wouldn't give in. She was my daughter, my responsibility, and I wanted her. That night I realized

I had to choose. I rang Don, her father and he said he'd be round to collect her.

'I'm not an aggressive person, but when Don arrived I attacked him physically. I said, "Congratulations. This is what your years of work have achieved." I was heartbroken. Two days later, he rang and asked to speak to Andy. Very odd, as he'd previously tried to ignore the fact that I had a husband. What he wanted was to meet Andy for a chat; exactly what Andy had wanted all along. They met in the pub, and it turned out Don didn't want Jenny living with him. Two days of having her there had already caused problems with the woman he was living with.

'So Jenny came home and I supposed it was a sort of turning point. Andy and I talked it over and decided that however hard he found it, he had to let me handle my daughter by myself without interfering. Ironically his mother died recently, and he is finding it very hard to accept his father's lady friend. If he, a mature adult, feels like this, how much harder must it be for a young girl?

'I don't blame Jenny. I blame her father. When I was no longer around for him to lean on emotionally, he leaned on her. He began to treat her more like a wife than a daughter, forcing her to share his worries and his unhappiness. Surprisingly she has never resented the woman who is now her step-mother. Possibly the biggest help to her was her father re-marrying. Someone else has taken the responsibility for him off Jenny's shoulders. She no longer has to protect him all the time.

'I won't say it's easy, even now. Because neither Andy nor I see any reason why he should support two kids who are not his – and whose father never lets them forget it – we have separate bank accounts. I have to go to work to support my children. I should get maintenance off my husband, but of course, he doesn't pay up. The last time I decided to fight for it and took him to court, Jenny refused to speak to me for weeks. It's not worth that.

'I feel bitter sometimes when I think of the enjoyment that has been taken out of our lives. Like the trip to America that was foreshadowed first by Don refusing to let Jenny go – we had to go to court – and then by her refusing to come because Daddy didn't like it. In the end she came, but so much of the fun had been drained from it. I still feel torn between two of the three people I love most. Thank goodness my younger daughter was young enough to welcome Andy and accept him as a smashing bonus, an extra Daddy.'

PART THREE

Teenage sexuality . . . a national obsession?

1

Whose obsession is it anyway?

'Meanwhile it was as though I had been dipped in hot oil, baked, dried, and hung throbbing on wires. Mysterious senses clicked into play overnight, possessed one in luxuriant order, and one's body seemed tilted out of all recognition by shifts in the balance of power. It was the time when the thighs seemed to burn like dry grass . . . when to lie face downwards in a summer field was to feel the earth's thrust go through you.'

Laurie Lee, *Cider with Rosie*

So much has been written about teenage sexuality that a visiting Martian would be forgiven for thinking that it is the sole obsession of earthlings between the ages of 12 and 20. And yet it's not – mostly they take it for granted.

Could it be that the mountain of words reflects more accurately parents' fears, doubts and preoccupations on their children's behalf, rather than the teenagers' own? As John Conger says in *Adolescence – Generation under Pressure*: 'The growing emphasis on openness and honesty is not evidence of increased preoccupation with sex, as many parents seem to think. It may well be that today's average adolescent, accepting sex as a natural part of life, is less preoccupied and concerned with it than his counterparts in earlier generations.'

Certainly parents are confused, and with reason. Over the past quarter of a century, since their adolescence, the rules of the game have changed dramatically. The moral ground has shifted beneath their feet. There is a new code of sexual conduct among the young that some of our moral watchdogs believe is turning the average suburb into Sodom and Gomorrah.

Most of today's parents were teenagers in the late 1950s and early 1960s – just before the Sixties started swinging. The rules were clearcut then, and society frowned on those who didn't at least make an effort to obey them. An unmarried mother (that all-embracing term 'single parent' had not been invented) would lose respect and bring disgrace on the family.

The pill was (if you'll pardon the expression) in its infancy. Family

Planning clinics asked for proof of marriage, and abortion was a backstreet nightmare for the poor and a Harley Street special for the wealthy. Good girls didn't – or if they did and were unlucky, they got married in a hurry.

The emphasis, you'll notice, was on girls – the age-old double standard. But if girls didn't, boys couldn't, the reasoning went. It's hard to imagine any parent relying on those reasons to preserve a daughter's purity nowadays. Even the Commandments don't hold the sway they once did.

'The difference,' said one father, 'is that we thought about it all the time and didn't know what to do about it. The lads today do it, forget about it and get on with the rest of life. Is that bad?'

'The difference,' said a mother, 'is that we had a lovely time day-dreaming about Elvis Presley or the Maths teacher before we faced reality. We enjoyed the flirting and the fantasising. The kids today may have sex by sixteen, but where's the romance?'

When today's girl says 'No' according to Agony Aunt Irma Kurtz (*Crisis – A Guide to your Emotions*), it is more likely to be because of fear of first-time pain or of 'not being good at it'.

She also picks up a worrying undercurrent. 'Just as we were under fierce pressure to stay virgins, the modern girl seems to be under peer pressure to lose her virginity.' Teenage girls write to tell Ms Kurtz that all their friends have 'done it' and they are so embarrassed at missing out, they have to pretend to be equally experienced.

Is it the price of equality, she muses, that girls will now boast about their sexual activity the way boys always have – and like the boys, will probably be exaggerating? You can't avoid the conclusion that Agony Columns, like Irma Kurtz's own in *Cosmopolitan*, exert a fair bit of pressure too, in their totally uncritical acceptance of teenage sexual relationships without a hint of moralising. Twenty years ago a girl writing to enquire if she should sleep with her boy-friend would have been strongly advised against it. The teen-age magazines, however, mindful of their very young readership, would probably still give the age-old answer. 'We have to be very conscious of the law and the age of consent,' says a young woman who answers problem letters for one of the best-selling teen-magazines.

'We point out to a girl under 16 that it is illegal for her to have sex with her boy-friend – but many of those who write to us are already doing so. What they want most is someone to talk it over with, because if they write to a magazine the implication is that they cannot talk to parents or anyone close to them. That's the saddest part of it.'

There is counter-pressure too, from organisations like the Responsible Society, which issues a leaflet for teenagers called 'Saying No Isn't Always Easy'.

This points to the hidden reasons why some teenagers embark on a sexual relationship very early. Often, says the writer, it is little to do with liberation, more to do with wanting to impress friends, to show parents you are not a child, or to prove you're neither repressed nor latently homosexual. All valid unemotive points to make a young person think twice. But why do some individuals who support such groups have to spoil it by going over the top, virtually accusing sex educators and counsellors of being in commercial league with the pill manufacturers and abortion clinics?

How are parents facing up to the new liberation? The attitudes vary dramatically. I met mums who rush their daughter off to be put on the pill at the first whisper of a boy-friend, and a mum who automatically puts her sons' visiting girl-friends in the same bedroom. (Every parent who *didn't* follow this practice claimed to know others who did).

I met those who were shocked by any manifestation of sexuality, like the mother who found a girlie-magazine in her son's room and tore it to shreds. 'What sort of expectations of women can it give him? It degrades us all.'

There were those who really would have preferred not to know. Among them, June, who came home early and disturbed her 16-year-old daughter in bed with her boy-friend. 'I wanted to run away – or die. My husband wanted to kill the lad. My daughter was cool as a cucumber. When the fuss died down, she said "I'm sorry, not for what we did, but for embarrassing you. You should have knocked." As soon as she left school, she moved in to live with her boyfriend's family. I feel we've lost her. We never felt completely at ease with her after what happened. I just wish we'd never found out.'

A few, like Marie, mother of two sons and two daughters, can say with total confidence. 'It has never crossed my mind that any of my children might be involved in under-age sex, even my youngest daughter, who is extremely rebellious and has been going out with boys since her early teens.'

'If young people have warmth and affection at home they don't need to go searching for it in sexual affairs, long before they are emotionally ready.'

And there was Bill, expressing yet another popular view: 'What right have people, like trendy sex educators, to tell kids that self-control is undesirable and the only choice is between intercourse and masturbation? It's a terrible pressure to put on a sensitive girl or a shy boy. They should be enjoying light-hearted friendships, instead of worrying about their sexual performance.'

There are a minority of parents who cannot understand what the talk and the tensions are about, but the vast majority feel a little uneasy about accepting their adolescents as sexual beings. Indeed, one father argued that this is a safeguard, a sort of natural incest taboo.

It's an area so fraught with tension that parents are apt to get bogged down and confuse their opinions with their gut-feelings. Called on to present an argument against embarking on an early sexual relationship, parents will usually resort to the practical – the threat of pregnancy, sexually-transmitted diseases, the medical question-mark hanging over the long-term use of the pill. The real reasons are probably far more primitive, emotional, illogical and tied up with old memories left over from their own adolescence.

Because it's a sin . . . Because sex outside marriage is not for decent people. (Or as one girl remembers her mother telling her at 15, 'Sex is for men, you know') . . . Because you're still my baby and I don't want you to grow up . . . Because I will be embarrassed and our relationship will change . . . Because it makes me feel old, or envious . . . Because you might get hurt.

Few people admit to such basic vulnerability, least of all to their teenagers. Parents have an image to preserve. It's not that they cherish ambitions for their children to become monks, nuns or Peter Pan. They want them to be popular, but pure too (particularly the girls!). They want them to get married, have children and live happily ever after. It's just that bit in between that makes them uncomfortable. It's what psychologist James Hemming, in his book, *You and your Adolescent* describes as 'the attempt to put sex into cold storage between puberty and marriage'.

Fathers have a particularly confusing time. They worry if their daughters are sexually active, and they worry if their sons are not. They also get kept in the dark rather a lot by their children, and often by their wives too.

Mothers tend to be the ones who find out what is really going on – by fair means or foul. But, as we all know a mother's place is in the wrong, and Clare Rayner, another of the ubiquitous Agony Aunts, describes (in *Related to Sex*) three typical specimens who are definitely not getting it right in her view.

There is 'the mother who eagerly discusses every detail of sexual activity (with her daughter) giving them a crash course in sexual gymnastics'. This thoroughly modern mum escorts her under-age daughter to pick up her supply of contraceptive pills, an act Ms Rayner views with suspicion. 'It's as though they want to share their child's sex life as a way of fulfilling a need of their own. If a girl is old enough to take the decision to use contraception she is old enough to get it herself.'

Specimen number Two 'talks about sex as though it happened to other women but never of course has it happened to her'. And there's a third category in Ms Rayner's book – the woman who never discusses sex, but isn't, as she thinks, making no statement. By her avoidance, she is suggesting it is not a subject fit for discussion in decent homes.

What hasn't changed over the years – only grown – is the basic problem of teenage sexuality: that young people are physically ready for such relationships (and indeed for parenthood) long before it is desirable, in our society, for them to embark on them. For a girl, the count-down to puberty can begin as early as eight, with the average girl having her first period at twelve. The average male reaches the peak of sexual energy, according to Kinsey, at 16 or 17.

There is an obvious conflict here between nature and civilization, since where most parents expect their teenagers to be peaking is in the classroom.

Some societies do things differently. There are cultures in which girls are married off on reaching puberty, and others in which adolescent sex is positively encouraged and erotic techniques short of intercourse, taught. Take the Kikuyu tribe in East Africa where 'Intimate contact between young people is considered right and proper and the very foundation stone upon which to build a race, morally, physically and mentally sound.'

What is feasible in darkest Africa may not be possible in Potters Bar, however, but do such anthropological comparisons have anything to teach us? James Hemming, thinks so: 'The error we seem to have made in our society is to associate sexual responsibility with the denial of sex. The reverse seems to be true. When sex is repressed it tends to break out in irresponsible and perverted forms. The unpleasanter deviations are much more common in the sexually inhibited societies.'

But psychologist Moira Hamlin poses another question. 'Isn't it possible that many parents – perhaps because of the way young people talk – assume their teenagers to be far more sexually sophisticated than they actually are?

Consequently they give them so much freedom without guidance that the kids are confused. They have nothing on which to base their own values or even to rebel against. The saddest thing about adolescent sexuality is the way parents get so hung up on the physical aspects but give no guidance about the emotions involved –

emotions that teenagers may not be able to handle.'

I'll let Irma Kurtz have the last word. Is a young girl prepared, she wonders, not only for the 'over-rated sacrifice' of losing her virginity, but to cope with the 'infidelity, jealousy, intimacy, distraction and disappointment' of a deeply emotional relationship?

'Girls are ready for sex physically long before it is fun to have it, and most youthful coupling is done in discomfort, in confusion and in a big hurry. Honestly, premature sexual intercourse is more likely to kill sexuality than to release it.'

2

Finding out

'I'm sure Mum doesn't know about sex. If she does she's never let me or my brother in on the secret. I've never seen her and the old man as much as hold hands. I often wonder if I'm a virgin birth – or if they found me under a gooseberry bush, which is what they told me, the only bit of sex education I've ever had at home.'

Richard (18)

Till I started researching this book, I suffered from a fairly common delusion – that modern mothers and fathers are uninhibited sophisticates who treat their children to intensive sex education from the cradle onwards; that they go bravely in, four-letter words and real biological terms flying, where no generation of parent has gone before. After all, we are all very open about sex these days, aren't we?

Well, it isn't true. Oh, undoubtedly there are pioneers out there, telling all, but mostly parents are still beating about the bush, evading the issues and leaving it to someone else. Just as they did 25 years ago. The 'someone else' tends to be school, where sex education can be all-embracing or very patchy depending on the whim of the head teacher.

'We get girls coming in pregnant,' said Peggy Wakelin, senior counsellor with the British Pregnancy Advisory Service, 'and you enquire if there was any sex education at their school. Sometimes you get an answer on the lines of: "Yes, but I was away that day."

'You can't, in a couple of lessons, teach the facts, let alone the strong feelings involved. These feelings often come as a shock to a teenager who has been brought up on facts alone. They are not prepared for them – and you get another teenage pregnancy.

'Of course it would be marvellous if all parents could be completely honest with their teenagers from the word go, but it just doesn't seem to be possible. The fact is that many regard their teenager developing into a sexual being as "letting us down" and teenagers are painfully aware of this. When a girl wants her pregnancy kept from her parents, it's the reason she always gives, letting them down.

'When parents do pass on the information, all too often they are giving out a double message – "this is what it's all about, but you are not to do it".

'I'll admit, as a mother myself, that the situation is not made easier by the fact that young people themselves at a certain stage don't want to discuss the subject with their parents.

'It is a very emotional subject for young people of around 13 or 14, or at whatever age they first arrive at puberty and start to get the sexual feelings that go with it. Their sensitivity makes it almost impossible to talk openly to them and it is at this stage that parents should give it a rest. Unfortunately, what often happens is that parents who have been very reticent spot the signs of puberty and panic. They suddenly realise that their children know very little and start force-feeding them the information they should have been picking up gradually over the years.

'Sex education is not something you suddenly introduce when you spot the first signs of impending puberty; nor do you sit a boy or girl down and deliver a solemn lecture on the facts of life. Ideally the topic is always openly discussed at home and questions are answered at a level appropriate to the child's age.'

To be fair most parents do pass on the basic physical essentials. Most girls are forewarned about menstruation (though a headmistress told me she still gets the occasional puzzled and distressed first-year, who has to be given a sanitary towel and an explanation by a teacher). Few, if any mothers-to-be will go into the maternity hospital, like the young mother of two teenagers I spoke to, with no idea of how the baby will arrive. If you have a television set or can read, it would be hard to maintain such innocence and ignorance.

It's the revelation of the finer details of procreation which puts a strain on parent–child communication. The Health Education Council estimate that only one in three parents 'get down to the details of having sex'. Some try passing on the information early, before mutual embarrassment becomes a problem, and are horrified to find the child didn't take it in or has forgotten at precisely the time they should be remembering.

A lot of parents, according to the teenagers themselves, never tell them anything and then, when they are 15 or 16, start talking to them as if they know it all. It's not at all unusual for parents who have never spoken about sexual relationships to start handing out contraceptive advice at 16. They assume the son or daughter will know exactly what they are talking about – and of course, nine times out of ten they are right.

The school playground, television, jokes, women's and girlie magazines are still the great sexual educators. Plus the school sex education programme, in which parents have enormous faith. Time and again, enquiring how parents had coped with the tricky subject, I was told; 'You don't need to tell them now; they get all that at school.'

Most parents are relieved to be rid of the burden; a few object strongly, insisting it was a parents' job, and would like to be able to withdraw their children from these lessons. 'They teach them plumbing and contraception, when they should be teaching ideals,' complained one mother. Others too felt that there was far too much emphasis on mechanics and the easy availability of contraception and none on the morality of sex and its context in a loving, preferably married, relationship. To be fair the people who work in the sex education and contraception field were intensely aware of the need to discuss feelings and emotions with young people. It was sometimes an uphill struggle particularly with teenage boys, who often regard 'feelings' as the last of the unmentionable words.

So how good and how valid is sex education in schools? Carol Lee who teaches the subject is in no doubt that it is essential. Not least, she insists (in *The Ostrich Position*) because teenagers know so little about the subject, contrary to what adults believe.

'Although they use four-letter words and sometimes fling out phrases about vibrators and jolly bags, this generally indicates sexual bravado rather than knowledge or experience. I have many times encountered people whose loud boasting covered a pathetic ignorance.'

She quotes the girl who talks nonchalantly about the pill but believes you insert it in your vagina, the boy who confuses the words 'lesbian' and 'prostitute' and 'the multitudes who believe that you get one go free (i.e. that you cannot get pregnant the first time).'

Miss Lee has an interesting theory about why the whole subject is so tricky for adults – not only parents, but many teachers – to approach with teenagers. It's because they speak different languages. Adults are limited to the few euphemisms and semi-medical terms they feel able to use; adolescents have evolved their own vocabulary, sometimes obscure and regional, but guaranteed to make the proverbial sailor blush.

However it hasn't removed the adolescent's embarrassment at using the words in public, which is why sex educators like Ms Lee often start a lesson by soliciting words for various activities and parts of the body, and boldly writing them on the blackboard. After the initial gasps and giggles, it de-mystifies the words and opens up discussion, she claims. As an outside tutor she is always careful to wipe the blackboard clean before the next teacher, mindful of language battles with head teachers and with colleagues while planning programmes.

Not only do colloquial terms cause adult blushes, the more blatant biological ones are considered unfit for the classroom. She recalls a six-month wrangle with the Health Education Council; over 'unacceptable' words: 'Explaining the process of menstruation without ever mentioning the word "vagina" is an exercise beyond my skills and aspirations!'

If the 13 and 14-year-olds that Carol Lee meets are uninformed, the slightly older group Miriam Stoppard 'sampled' in *Talking Sex* sound quite the opposite. They showed no qualms, it seems, about answering Dr Stoppard's somewhat impertinent questions. There is a touch of voyeurism in the exercise, but it can be argued that it is reassuring for a teenager reading the book to know that he or she is not alone or odd whatever he or she is doing. Only the quieter teenager, not contemplating quite so busy a sex life, might feel a bit out of it!

If you want to know what teenagers are doing and how they feel about it, the statistics, according to Miriam Stoppard break down as follows. One in three boys masturbates two or three times a week; the same number do so once weekly. It is considered an acceptable activity among boys, tolerated even by adults. Only half as many girls numbered it among their activities.

Fantasising was another popular pastime. Boys' fantasies tended to be over nude female bodies, but girls were more romantic, more specific and always had a real boy in mind.

Half the boys had (or told Dr Stoppard they had) intercourse before the age of 18. They claimed generally to find these early experiences rewarding but suffered from fears that they were expected to be more knowledgeable and experienced than they were.

Girls, on the other hand, expected a lot from the experience and were often let down – to the extent that they became worried there was something wrong with them. The spoilsports here were guilt and the suspicion that the boy was not interested in their feelings but in 'only one thing'. Many girls admitted to battling with a dilemma their mothers might recall – how to say no to a boy without losing him. They were afraid of getting a reputation as a tease or alternatively as a prude, and terrified of being out of step with what the other girls in their crowd appear to be doing.

Dr Stoppard asked them about petting too – and found that girls believed it should be kept for 'when you love a boy' whereas boys hoped it would occur on the first or second date. The boys also believed it was something they should be into by the age of 15, whereas the girls thought age was irrelevant, and it depended on your feelings for a particular boy. Four out of five boys felt it was okay to 'go the whole way', but only half the girls agreed with them.

Parents were the subject of much discussion. Two-thirds of boys and girls felt unable to be open with their parents about sex. In general this wasn't because parents were openly disapproving; more that they never brought up the subject and the kids didn't know how to broach it. They took the silence as disapproval.

A quarter of the sample guessed that their parents had a good idea of how sexually experienced they were. Many felt parents didn't want to know; some even attempted to drop snippets of information into their parents apparently reluctant ears.

One in ten told parents everything about their sex lives; one in five told their parents the bits they thought would be acceptable; while the same number never mentioned sex at home. About half agreed that they could talk to parents about sex in a general way, but not subjectively, about themselves.

'If I told them how I really felt, they would stop trusting me,' was a typical reason given for keeping mum around Mum – and more particularly, Dad. Dads in Dr Stoppard's survey were a dead loss as confidants. Both boys and girls who did talk about sex, did so to their mother; the most openness being between mother and daughters. The worst? Fathers and daughters. 'My Dad thinks I'm going to get pregnant all the time,' one complained.

The overall feeling to emerge from *Talking Sex* is that girls have a harder time of it, sexually speaking. Carol Lee incidentally refutes this from her classroom experience. If anything she says, her experience suggests it is the other way round, but that boys like to appear cool, worldly and able to cope when questioned.

3

'Boys don't get pregnant'

'We always seem to look at teenage sex as a problem of unwanted pregnancies, and since it is girls who become pregnant, we try to solve it by concentrating on girls alone.'

Susie Hayman, of The Family Planning Association and
The Brook Centre

Adolescent boys have their own sexual fear and uncertainties though they take some digging out because of the shield of bravado used to hide them. They may discuss the most intimate sexual details in the most brutally frank language, but find it impossible to admit to caring for a girl. They may boast about sexual conquests but in reality be too shy to make the smallest approach. They may strut around as if they were God's gift to teenage womankind but spend secret, agonised hours worrying over something like the size of their penis, the strength of their muscles or the persistence of their acne.

Nobody has much sympathy for them. Whereas efforts are made to prepare girls for dramatic developments like menstruation, male adolescent phenomena such as embarrassingly unpredictable erections and wet dreams are the subject of ribald humour. Mostly boys will join in with the joke – when it's against someone else. Peer pressure and group bravado dictate that they appear informed, experienced and cool.

Ignorance (i.e. innocence) is considered distinctly wet among boys, and they are less likely to form the close best-friendships girls go in for, where all secrets can be shared. Consequently, some boys would rather suffer in silence than ask the simple questions that relieve the worry, but reveal their ignorance.

The problem is that if they don't find out from friends and don't like to ask at school, they have no-one to ask. Girls talk to mothers more readily than boys talk to fathers or mothers. They read teenage and women's magazines, which do a surprisingly thorough job of discussing female problems; and if really concerned they can write to the ubiquitous Agony Aunt.

Girls, getting in the deep end in a sexual relationship, are likely to seek help at a birth control clinic. And they are not necessarily only there for the pill. As Susie Hayman, who has been Press Information Officer for both the Brook Centre and the FPA, points out, when they find a sympathetic ear, the girls often want to talk about other problems. 'They may want to chat about family quarrels, fears about their bodies, sexual doubts and emotional worries. Where do boys go for such reassurance?'

Where indeed? Taking this as a starting point, Ms Hayman makes a convincing case for educating and encouraging boys to use such clinics. Not only for the counselling help they may pick up there, naturally, but to persuade them to take their share of responsibility in a sexual relationship.

Birth control clinics concentrate almost exclusively on girls. School sex education tends to have a heavy bias towards them too. The result, Susie Hayman fears, is: 'The impression young men get is that the problems, the consequences, the emotional entanglements are a feminine preserve. Men are left feeling that their role is as the predator, snatching selfish pleasure, boasting among themselves, the instant experts who never have any self-doubts.

'Naturally, most find their feelings and the image of what is "manly" clash, but they hide their worries, each believing they are unique and abnormal.'

No-one doubts that the reluctance of boys to take responsibility has a bearing on the high number of teenage pregnancies. Susie Hayman predicts another long-term effect. 'By distancing themselves from responsibility, boys also distance themselves from emotional involvement. Sex becomes an arena in which to score points, not a private give-and-take of feelings.'

Birth control clinics, when they get young men in, are not sure what to do with them. A 1981 survey shows that boys stand only a 50-50 chance of getting advice and help there. Sheila Schüler of Brook admits: 'We occasionally get teenage boys coming in and we try to treat them with the same sensitivity we give to girls but, honestly, it is very hard to take them seriously.

'No girl ever comes in here for a joke – not when she has to go through the process of history-taking and an internal examination, but there's no such hassle for boys. You never know if they are serious and hiding it with bravado, or if they are just there for a giggle. They almost invariably come with a group of mates and there's a lot of playing around and cheeking us. Yet sometimes when you get one of them alone, he will tell you about his girl-friend and turn out to be quite shy.'

The professionals are making efforts to practise equality. Parents rarely try. Even in liberal households, there is often one rule for the boys and another for the girls. Many are surprised you would even query it.

'Of course I treat my daughter differently from my son when it comes to freedom and the opposite sex,' said one father. 'Girls *are* different. Boys don't get pregnant.'

The girls lose out on this double standard because they are deprived of freedom. But the boys lose out too because they are given so little scope for expressing the more sensitive side of their nature. Ultimately, of course, we all lose out in breeding a generation of macho men. Carol Lee is frequently alarmed by the attitudes among 14 and 15-year-old boys . . . boys who believe 'that aggression is necessary to virility and that women enjoy it'. At its most extreme, she is talking about rape.

'For teenage boys, sexual experience is mainly something to be cheered about and boasted of,' she says. 'It requires a fair amount of work to introduce them to the idea of rape as violation and a tragedy.'

To try and illustrate the point, Ms Lee is in the habit of play-acting a mock trial in the classroom. The 15-year-old rape victim faces the alleged rapist and the rest of the class take the roles of defence, prosecution, judge and jury. The interesting thing to come out of these little courtroom dramas is that no boy has ever been found guilty.

Carol Lee points out that if we want to stop male violence towards women and do something about the painful lack of understanding between the sexes that continues long after the classroom play-acting has ended, adolescence is where we have to start.

How? By unearthing the emotions that teenage boys have buried beneath the layers of indifference and aggression, and persuading them that they are nothing to be ashamed of. By talking less about the physical aspects of sex and more about relationships, caring, understanding, liking and loving. All words that stick in the throat of the average adolescent boy.

Are boys different? Psychologist and expert on this age group, John Conger: 'In early adolescence, at least, for reasons which we do not entirely understand – although psychological (including hormonal) and psychological factors are probably both involved – boys are more conscious of specifically sexual impulses than girls, and find them harder to deny. Sexual drive among girls is likely to be more diffuse and ambiguous and more intertwined with other needs, such as love, self-esteem, reassurance and affection.'

Or, to put it statistically, quoting a survey done by Dr Michael Schofield; 42 per cent of girls gave 'love' as a reason for having intercourse. Only 10 per cent of boys gave that reason, but 45 per cent of them said 'sexual desire'. How much of the answer is inspired by biology and how much by conditioning is hard to guess.

Yes, boys are different, but behind the mask, maybe not as different as they pretend.

4

The schoolgirl, the pill and the right to know

'Any woman who says her fifteen-year-old daughter tells her everything is naïve or lying.'

Diane Munday, British Pregnancy
Advisory Service

One of the biggest controversies of the 1980s has centred around one small question – if a girl under sixteen asks to be prescribed the contraceptive pill, should the doctor *have* to inform her parents?

Hiding within that question are all sorts of other issues – legal and emotional. If the age of consent is sixteen, surely it is making a mockery of the law to prescribe contraceptives for a girl who is younger? If a parent's permission is sought in other medical matters, why miss this one out? When must a parent relinquish the power and responsibility to make moral decisions on a child's behalf? Is the state poking its nose into matters that should concern the family? Whose child is it anyway? And when does a child cease to be a child in anything more than legal terms, and take responsibility for its own decisions and actions?

The history of the issue dates back to 1974, when the Department of Health and Social Security acknowledged that the soaring birth and abortion figures for under-16s demanded some action.

Recommendations were made that contraceptives should be available 'to young people at risk of pregnancy regardless of age'. Doctors and other professionals were reassured that they were not breaking the law in prescribing without parental permission, though it was stressed that they should try to persuade the girls either to tell their parents or allow someone else to do so on their behalf.

The plan was a success (though many parents might take issue with that). Girls who would probably have risked pregnancy had their parents been involved, came forward to ask for advice and help at clinics and doctors' surgeries. The figures for pregnancy and abortion in young girls have never been so high since.

The DHSS move didn't please everyone. There has been growing disquiet among parents. A movement dedicated to getting the "confidentiality" guidelines revoked has grown up. It is understandable, if unrealistic. No parent actually approves of under-age sex. Many are not over-enthusiastic about it as a pastime for their 16 or 17-year-olds either.

The issue of course is not really about the acceptability of contraception (though there remains a medical question-mark over the safety of long-term use of the pill), but about the acceptability of teenage sex. As Sheila Schüler points out, 'on the pill' has become the polite euphemism for 'having sex'. And that's what parents find hard to accept.

The combination of teenage and sex in a newspaper headline has never done anything to harm sales, and the media has blown the issue up out of proportion. There are not hordes of Lolitas queuing up for their supply of pills on the way home from school.

In a year, the Family Planning Association sees 14,000 girls under sixteen, an average of eight girls per clinic. This represents 1 per cent of the country's 13–15-year-old girls. The Brook Centre estimates that 3½ per cent of their clients are under 16; the majority of these being 15.

'14-year-olds are rare enough to cause comment,' said Sheila Schüler. 'A 13-year-old is a true rarity and almost always a girl in care, brought along by a social worker.'

Brook offers confidentiality at any age, but young girls are encouraged to tell parents and counselled at length so that they can understand the problems and practicalities of trying to keep their pill-taking secret. The majority of girls say that they will tell their parents, but in their own time . . . and do.

Sheila Schüler, Birmingham Brook: 'Our team, which interviews every new client consists of a doctor, a nurse, a social worker and the receptionist – who plays a crucial role as the first person clients encounter. With a young girl who does not want her parents to know, the social worker's job is to point out to her what this secrecy will actually mean. Has she ever kept a secret from Mum before? Does she realize how attempting to might affect their relationship?

'Obviously it would be better if they could at least tell their mothers. Fathers seem to be out of the question. Ask a girl what their father would think and they usually say, "He'd kill me". If you delve a little deeper however, you'll find a clue that father mightn't be so shocked. One girl said that when something a bit saucy was said on television, her father would say, "You shouldn't be laughing at this, you shouldn't understand it." But his attitude was jovial, not disapproving. I think a lot of parents know, or suspect, their children are having sex, but don't or can't talk about it. Once you know, it makes for all sort of embarrassments. Are you supposed to provide them with time and privacy for their relationship? Do you put them sleeping in the same room? It is so much easier to hide your head in the sand and pretend it doesn't exist. Very few parents can talk freely to their children about sex.

'Of course, some parents do find out their daughter is secretly on the pill. Our receptionist fields the occasional phone-call from an irate parent, usually Mum. Sometimes they pretend to be the daughter checking when her next appointment is. Confidentiality is not only a matter of not writing a letter to the family doctor or the parents. You have to learn to speak to people without giving anything away.

'Usually it is a mother who has found the pills and our phone number. Without admitting anything you try to talk to her and let her talk. Often you'll find she is having her own problems, having a difficult time with her children's teenage years. She is angry and distressed and feels someone is taking over from her in her daughter's life. Maybe they have been bosom pals who discussed everything. Now it seems her daughter has found another life, and discarded her. It seems bewildering and very hurtful. They are hurt because she is on the pill and because she didn't tell them. The last thing the girls want is for their mother to find out from someone else. Most of them feel they will tell her when they are ready.

'I usually suggest to the mother that she takes the matter up with her daughter and phones me again if she wants to talk or come in. Again, all in a very vague way, though you know you're not fooling anyone, really. Quite often they will tell you that talking to you has been a great help.

'There is so much more involved in your child's developing sexuality than whether or not they are using a contraceptive, isn't there? Jealousy that someone has taken your child from you; sadness and a bit of envy for a mother that romance is dead for her and it is all starting for her daughter; a vague feeling that it is not nice. Or that it is all right for other people's teenagers but not for yours. "I'm on the pill" has become a euphemism for "I'm having a sexual relationship". It's the way girls tell their mother, when they do.

'What strikes me listening to the debates about teenage sexuality is that they all start from the basic premise – that what we are discussing is a bad thing. That a loving relationship between two young people, in which sex plays a part, is wrong. It's the views on how to cope with it which differ.

'I'd hesitate to stand up in public and ask this – but is it wrong? Couldn't it be, that like Romeo and Juliet, it could be very beautiful as long as there are no babies?

'After all it is acceptable in some cultures. Not promiscuity, if that means sleeping with several partners without any deep feelings involved, but I see no evidence at all that girls who go on the pill in their teens are promiscuous. On the contrary, it is all to do with romance and their feelings for one boy.

'If that relationship ends, they stop taking the pill. It's a sign of commitment to one boy, rather like an engagement ring used to be. I realise I am talking about a particular sort of person, not every girl. But it takes a pretty responsible and mature young girl to seek out an agency like this and talk to the numerous people involved about so personal a matter.'

Postscript: In December 1984, three Lord Justices of Appeal backed the view of Mrs Victoria Gillick that it is illegal for doctors to give contraceptive advice or treatment to girls under 16 without parental consent. The BMA immediately asked the Department of Health to exercise the right of appeal to the Lords. A spokesman said, 'Nothing should be put in the way of encouraging a young girl in these circumstances from seeing a doctor.'

A spokesman for the Brook Advisory Service in Birmingham added: 'The ruling has confused the issue even further. For instance it allows doctors to prescribe in emergency, but gives no definition of the word. We are not certain where we stand even with giving advice.

The last thing we want though is for young girls to lose their trust in us and have nowhere to turn for help. Any girl who comes to see us, whatever the outcome, whether we prescribe or not, can be assured of complete confidentiality.'

5

Teenage mums

Not all pregnant girls opt for abortion, by any means. Several choose to have the baby and then face the choice of bringing it up single-handed or considering adoption. There is often pressure from older people, parents included, to 'do the sensible thing' – which means termination.

Sometimes this pressure comes as a bolt out of the blue. Pat, pregnant at 16, was horrified when her mother wanted her to have an abortion. 'I couldn't believe it. I'd been brought up to believe abortion was wrong, but when someone in the family was in trouble, it seems the rules changed.'

Two of the teenage mothers-to-be I spoke to were awaiting the birth of their babies in a comfortable, but fairly basic terraced house, run for that purpose by LIFE, the anti-abortion group. The group helps women of any age in this position. Pat, however, had another option. She married her boyfriend – again with less than enthusiastic support from her family.

'It's funny,' a marriage guidance counsellor told me, 'A few years back, parents would be holding a shotgun to the lad's head, forcing the pair to the altar at all costs. Now it's the parents trying to persuade the daughter that she doesn't have to get married, and the young people insisting they want to.'

But can a girl who is little more than a child herself cope with motherhood? Psychologist Moira Hamlin has doubts. Even in her late teens, she says, a girl has not fully negotiated the stages of adolescence. To avoid them, by taking on marriage and motherhood, can lead to emotional damage. Indeed, to become a fully separate, independent adult, she will have to go through adolescence at some stage – which might explain some of the 30-year-old adolescents you see around.

'And the process is just as painful at 30 as at 16,' Moira says.

Teenage marriages have a sad habit of ending up in the divorce courts, because they so often start under the handicap of pregnancy, poor housing and little money. The NSPCC lists too-early parenthood as a major factor in baby-battering.

'The problem here,' explains Moira Hamlin, 'is that a parent has to push away his or her own needs in favour of the baby's needs. You may want to sleep, but if the baby wants to be fed, you have to get up. With a very young mother or father, the effect is of two competing babies. The anger and resentment can build up to a dangerous level.

'I don't believe in instinctive mothering. As mothers, we all do things we learned – consciously or unconsciously – from our own mothers. This experience, how well or how poorly a girl was mothered herself, is a big factor in determining what sort of mother she will be. It's particularly true in teenage girls.

'You just have to hope that they know what a baby is – that they don't just want a doll to play with or something to keep them occupied because they haven't a job. Motherhood *is* a job, a job for life.'

Peta, as pretty as a Mothercare cover-girl in her dainty white shoes and red maternity dress. Not for this 18-year-old, the couldn't-care-less lethargy about appearance that strikes many mothers-to-be in the last weeks of pregnancy. She is childlike and chatty, but inevitably the chat leads back to a nightmare childhood and early adolescence that took her into a Children's Home at 14:

'It was lovely in the Home. They bought us new shoes and clothes – I love dressing up and looking pretty – and we were taken out and allowed to wear make-up. I never wanted to go home again.'

Her real home was a big city overspill estate, with an older brother and two sisters, one younger than Peta. Her father worked nights and had to have quiet during the day. Peta hardly ever saw him. 'To this day I cannot talk to him. I get tongue-tied in his company because he is a stranger. It's very strange, he never took part in our lives. He seemed to live his life in one room and Mum kept us in the other room or the kitchen. We went to bed really early, at around the time he went to work. A bit later Mum went out to play bingo.

'Mum used to beat us quite a lot. She would shut the kitchen door, so that my father couldn't hear. She could always find something we'd done wrong. I just accepted it. I didn't know anyone else's life was much different. I mean, at school you'd hear someone say "My Mum would kill me if she found out" or "My Dad belted me when I came in late last night." I didn't really know there was a difference between what they were talking about and what happened in our house. You don't want to be different, do you? When you get into your teens you try even harder to be just like everybody else.

'It came out when I was 14. I remember I was in the shower at school, after games, and suddenly I noticed the way the other girls were staring at my back. I knew it was sore because I'd just had a beating, but I didn't know how bad it looked. They started pointing and gasping and somebody fetched a teacher.

'Things started moving after that. A social worker came to school to see me. Then he came round to the house. I was terrified. I couldn't speak while my Dad was in the room – I didn't want to get her into trouble with him or with the authorities. I remember the social worker saying, "I think they will have to go into care," and my mother saying, "Yes, maybe that's the best thing."'

Peta went back home at 16. 'I'd been visiting my Mum for weekends and she used to cry and say she missed me and wanted me back. I'd been home a couple of weeks and it started again – not the beatings, but the rows, her bossing me about. I was over the road chatting to my mates one light summer night and she came over and dragged me back inside. It was really embarrassing. I tried talking to her, saying, 'I'm 16, I'm old enough to do these things," but she would shout me down and I'd just start to cry. I could never stand up to her.

'I have tried talking to her about the way she used to hit us, but she'd just say, "What's past is past. I don't want to talk about that now." I sometimes think she hated me. I know she was jealous of me. My Mum is beautiful even now, but people say I'm pretty too. When I started to get pretty, she got really nasty to me. I've never worn much make-up but if a mate gave me blusher or mascara and I put in on, she'd say I looked stupid or I looked like a tart and make me take it off. If men whistled when we were in the street, she would think it was at her. If she could see it was me, she'd turn very nasty. When I went home, she was jealous of the way my little sister always wanted me instead of her.

'My Mum never told me anything about sex or the facts of life. My first period, I didn't know what was happening to me. I didn't know where the blood was coming from. A teacher had to tell me and show me what a sanitary towel was.

'Girls at school were always talking about what they had done with their boy-friends and then they'd turn and say "What about you, Peta?" It wasn't very hard to invent a few stories from what I'd heard the others say, but the truth is I wasn't interested in lads. It would have been a waste of time if I was. There were a few who were interested in me, but when they came to call for me, my Dad told them to stay away from his daughter. He frightened them off.

'The only time anything was mentioned on the subject was when I went back home after being in care. My Mum started to say something about going on the pill. I was really shocked. I hated anything like that – and anyway, I didn't even have a boy-friend.'

A few months later however, Peta had left home, unable to

confidante, accepting his sexual nature in a way his parents could not.

'The way my parents behaved you'd have thought I wanted to be gay just to spite them. I didn't know till I met Andrew. I'd had girl-friends. Andrew used to hang around me. Some of the other lads started making a joke of it, saying he had a crush on me. I was intrigued I suppose, and interested, though I hadn't pinned a label on myself then.

'He started coming round to my house; one night he stayed. We got talking about our feelings and, well, the inevitable happened. We just accepted that we had a relationship. There was no big drama till his auntie got wind of it. I've never understood why there was such a fuss. I mean, it's a known fact that all boys – all human beings – go through a homosexual phase.'

His mother's rejection was treated seriously enough for Nicky to spend the next three months in an assessment centre, where his behaviour deteriorated to such an extent that he was sent to a remand school.

'I've never felt so unhappy as I did during those first three months. My mother never came to see me. I kept wondering if I'd ever see my family again and what I could do to put things right. I doubted I could change and go straight. By now I knew what I was. I felt life had treated me unfairly all round. I played up to get back at everyone, though in the end of course, I was the one who got hurt.'

The couple of years after leaving school and joining the dole queue were a round of short-lived gay relationships, interspersed with short stays at home, where he had been tentatively accepted back. There was even an attempt at a serious relationship with a girl, but that only convinced him that he did not belong in the 'straight world'.

A year ago, after a seemingly permanent break with home, he bumped into his father in the street. 'For the first time I really told him what I think of him and Mum . . . that they had never tried to understand me. It was always what I'd put them through, not what I was going through trying to come to terms with being gay. They'd never tried to see it from my side. I'd been rejected for being myself. By this time you see, I had accepted it. I wasn't bothered or ashamed at all. What is there to be ashamed of? It's just something that's in you; it's part of you.

'It was a sort of breakthrough somehow. My Dad said he wanted me to keep in touch and told me to come home whenever I wanted to. It's odd. With my gay friends, it's nearly always the mother who accepted it easier, but not mine.

'My father, now, I think he understands what I've been through.

We are closer than we've been since I was a kid. Not that we sit around discussing the gay scene or my relationships! Far from it. I've tried to talk about that side of myself to him, but he changes the subject. He'd rather we kept to chat about telly programmes or football. But we get on okay, considering everything. I think he's just puzzled that a son of his could turn out gay when he's always been 100 per cent macho himself!

'My mother's attitude has always been more one of anger and disgust. She is very, very old-fashioned. The only way she can accept me is by blotting the truth out of her mind. When I have been living with someone, she makes a point of saying "the man you are staying with," or "sharing a flat with". She will not allow herself to admit that the relationship is anything more than flat-mates. She couldn't accept that and continue to see me.

'The sad thing about that is that if one day I meet the right person and want to settle down, I will never be able to take him home and introduce him honestly to the family. I'll always have to put on an act, live a little lie.

'The person I could introduce him to is Brenda, my older sister. She didn't know about me being gay till last year – my parents had done everything in their power to keep it from her and the rest of the family.

'I just figured that sooner or later somebody would go up to her and ask if she knew her brother was a raving queer. It seemed easier to tell her the truth myself, so I invited her round to my flat and told her. She wasn't shocked. Her view is that whatever I am or whatever I did, short of murder, I am still her brother and she'd stick by me.

'Now when I'm down, she's the one I ring up for a chat. She's like an Agony Aunt, always ready to give advice on emotional problems. I suppose she treats me no differently than if I was her kid brother having girl-friend trouble. The fact that it's boy-friend trouble hasn't thrown her in the least.

'That's how I'd have liked my parents to react. I'd like them to have reassured me that I was still their son and they loved me. Okay, I feel I have a family still. I'm getting a flat of my own soon, as good as I can afford it on my dole money, and they've been round to see it; I can go out for a drink with Dad. But I can't be honest with them. There's a barrier that I doubt will ever go.

'When I was about 16 and having all the aggro with my parents, I used to say I didn't give a damm what they thought. But you do care, because, at the end of the day, your parents are the only true friends you have.

'This is particularly true when you're gay. There is a gay "underground" and it can be vicious. Young gay boys are at the mercy of unscrupulous older men at least as much as any young girl. Get in with the wrong company and you are as likely to be used and abused in the same way.

'Of course you don't have to involve yourself with the worse elements of the gay scene – there are many good, decent people who happen to be homosexual. But when you feel insecure and lonely, when your family reject you, you can very easily find yourself lured in. It's one way of having friends; sometimes it seems the only way.'

Nora, a widow, the mother of three sons and a younger daughter. She is a pillar of the village community, a stalwart of the parish council.

The teenage years of her two older boys were happy and uneventful. Both now have good jobs and are happily and conventionally married. Brian, the youngest son, however was different. 'There were no girl-friends around, although he was – and is – a handsome boy and girls were always chasing him,' Nora remembers. 'His relationship with boys seemed somehow closer that the usual casual friendships of teenage boys. You notice these things at the time, but they hold no significance.

'It's the little things that should have alerted me, like being shown a pile of photographs of him and his friends on holiday – and realising that there were only men in the picture, no girls. It strikes a brief discordant note, but you put it out of your mind. It was still a complete shock when Brian told me he was homosexual.'

Brian 'came out' (though Nora had never heard this expression at the time) after being involved in a car accident. 'He was shaken up and distraught. There was police involvement and I suppose he realised that all sorts of routine questions about where he was going would have to be answered. There was a good chance that the truth would emerge and Brian didn't want us to find out from someone other than himself.

'So he told us, his father and myself. He'd known for certain since he was 16 and had suspected it before. He said he'd been trying to find the right time to tell me but he could never get round to it. It was a relief that the time was forced on him.

'It is almost impossible to describe the shock. It's like a loss, a bereavement. You feel such anguish and bewilderment and guilt. Where had I gone wrong? What had I done to cause this? And you are so ignorant. I knew absolutely nothing about gay people or their lives. Why should I? I was heterosexual, so I assumed everyone else I knew was too.

'I put on an act, tried to hide how shocked I was. To show Brian how upset I was would have made it even harder for him, and he was so distraught. I assured him it would make no difference, that we'd still be close. We were – and are, thank goodness – very close.

'It was different for his father. He frowned on the whole thing, and although, on the surface he came round to accepting it, I believe that at a deeper level he never did. I was never able to talk publicly about it while my husband was alive, because he could not cope with anyone else knowing. My husband was a military man, you see. He'd had it drummed into him that homosexuality was a crime and totally unnatural. He never really let go of that idea.

'When your son or daughter tells you they are gay, you are plunged into a secret world against your will. You wonder what the neighbours and the relatives will say. No, that's not quite true . . . you think you know what they will say. You think they will reject you. You can't talk to anyone because you daren't let anyone else know. Sometimes you can't even talk to your husband or wife, because they can't bring themselves to discuss it. You are totally isolated.

'I turned first to the vicar, then the doctor. They were sympathetic, but they didn't know what to say to me. It was outside their experience too. Ignorant as I then was, what I wanted was for the doctor to cure Brian. I went to see a naval surgeon I knew. I thought at least he was used to dealing with men, so it couldn't be totally new to him.

'It wasn't and he was marvellous. He told me all he knew and reassured me that though the cause of homosexuality was not known, it was certainly nothing I had done. He also got rid of the notion I had that getting Brian to a good psychiatrist would make him heterosexual.

'By coincidence, listening to the radio, I heard Rose Robertson, who founded Parents Enquiry speaking. She too was the mother of a gay son and had been through all the doubts and fears that I had. She talked of starting this self-help group, so that a parent who had discovered her child was homosexual could contact another for support – or just for a chat.

'I involved myself with Parents Enquiry and have been involved ever since. It was my way of coping, by turning something negative into something positive. And of course it meant that I was learning about the gay world and staying part of my son's life.

'Brian has a steady, stable relationship now and is quite open with his friends and colleagues. He doesn't live near home but he visits and brings his friend. I treat the young man in the same way that I treat the wives of my other two sons, as part of the family. To be honest, it was a little difficult at first. I wasn't sure of the etiquette – you know, whether I should put them in the same room or what.

'Initially the only person I told inside the family was my eldest son. The second son and my daughter, Brian told himself, in his own time. They took it very well. They are a different, more liberal generation. Let's hope they will stay that way and not become as set in their attitudes to their children as my generation.

'I only told my sister a year ago. She admitted that she had suspected for some time. People do guess, you know. They ask questions about girl-friends and I suppose you stall, not liking to tell either the truth or a bare-faced lie. It probably shows. Most people are not as shocked as you think they will be, but it is hard to get that across to someone who rings up, convinced that they are the parent of the only homosexual in the world.

'A woman rings me regularly now. She is on the verge of a nervous breakdown, because neither she nor her husband can accept their son's homosexuality. She is sure people will find out and shun them. I try to remind her that he is still the son she loved when she didn't know, and that he is able-bodied and healthy, which you should always be thankful for. He's just a bit different, in the same way that one child has blue eyes and one has brown. And isn't it even worse if your child doesn't trust you sufficiently to tell you, and the barrier is between you for life?

'This woman's son talks to me too. He doesn't know what to say to his mother any more. What can he say, except to tell her that he loves her and that he hasn't changed?

'I often think back to all the signals that I ignored. A mother has a sixth sense about these sort of things, but it seems easier at the time to ignore it. It's funny really – I saw myself as a broad-minded liberal mother, you know. When he was eighteen, Brian went off to Greece in an old Dormobile with a beautiful girl.

'I assumed they would be sleeping together and prided myself on not minding. I suppose I was relieved after my little suspicions. It was only when she did not appear on the photographs he sent home, that the doubts began to niggle again. The girl knew the truth all along apparently. That was the reason she was going with him, because he was safe.'

PART FOUR
Problems

1

Unemployment

Ironically, unemployed young people, those under 18, were quite thin on the ground. This is the direct result of a new enthusiasm for staying on at school (often because the alternative seems so uninviting) and of the government's training and work experience schemes, YTS. This scoops up the majority of school leavers. For some it offers the hope of a job at the end of the year; for others it postpones the dole queue.

Limited or non-existent experience of life on the dole produced a variety of reactions to questions about employment hopes. Many still at school were optimistically chirpy that they would be different.

'*Someone* has to get the jobs that are going,' said one 16-year-old girl who had turned down the offer of a shop job to take a vocational college course. She was only averagely-academic, but convinced that with the right approach she would not be out of work.

A 17-year-old boy agreed with her.

'I went on a Youth Employment Scheme, because my Mum nagged me to do it. I hated it. I felt like cheap labour and I packed it in after a week.

'I had no ambition or anything. I hardly thought about work till the day I left school – my parents were the ones who worried about it. I figured I'd probably doss around for a couple of years. It sounded okay. Anyway, someone told me about a job going at a meat-packing place, so I thought I might as well go and ask for the job.

'I walked in and asked to see the boss – I'm fairly confident. He never asked to see my CSEs. He took me on because, he said afterwards, he liked my attitude. He didn't think much of kids who left it to someone else to find them work instead of coming in and asking. I suppose a lot of kids reckon jobs like mine are not good enough for them.'

There was a sprinkling of what one Careers Teacher described as 'the no-hopers', particularly among the less academic. It wasn't, the teacher explained, that he thought they had no hope. He encouraged them to believe that the situation could only get better and good exam results would help them get the jobs when they re-appeared. But the kids themselves couldn't see it that way.

'A lot of my mates haven't bothered taking exams,' said one 15-year-old. 'What's the point of knocking yourself out to get a few CSEs, when there are real swots with A-levels who can't find work?'

What were he and his friends hoping to do after school, I asked another boy. 'I don't ask anyone else,' he said. 'You get a reputation as a real pain in the neck if you sit around discussing the job situation. I mean, we know there aren't many jobs, and we're all in the same boat, so what is there to talk about? It seems a long way off, though I'll be leaving school next year. They try to talk you into staying on for the Sixth Form, but what's the point? You'll be two years older and still unemployed.'

A lot of the teenagers are aware that adults see unemployment as a disgrace. 'I do try for jobs. I go down the Job Centre all the time,' said a 17-year-old girl defensively. 'I've had a few interviews, but whatever I do, my Mum doesn't believe I'm trying. She says: "I don't understand it. You're good enough to do any of these jobs. You just don't show enough interest."'

'I never know the right thing to say at interviews. I wish they'd taught us more at school about talking to people and having confidence, instead of stuffing us with Maths. They don't really prepare you.'

There is still a faint disbelief among parents – themselves in work since they were 15 or 16 – that there are no jobs. Endless rows blow up over the teenager who is 'not looking hard enough'. 'They just sit back and accept the situation,' one father complained.

The mother of an 18-year-old unemployed girl said: 'It's driving me mad having her under my feet, and she's so bored. You have to subsidise her because the dole doesn't go far and she dresses like she's earning a top secretary's wage. It's always "Can I have money for this, or that?" It's ridiculous when you think she's an adult and you're supporting her. It's not the normal sort of relationship you have with a person that age.'

The hard face of realism, according to a Youth Employment Officer in a major city, is that only one in ten of the 16-year-old school leavers she sees is lucky enough to get a permanent 'no-strings' job. 'And they find it themselves, through determination, exceptional personality or someone they know,' she said. The rest go on to courses or the dole or government schemes – which may or may not have a job at the end of them. Others with no plans for higher education, stay on at school for something to do, and to clock up a few more CSEs or O-levels.

The Government survey *Young People in the 80s* (HMSO 1983) found, among teenagers, 'a great deal of uncertainty and unwilling-ness to confront the issue of unemployment . . . no very clear information as to the kind of jobs looked for emerged . . . a considerable proportion appeared to have little or no idea what they wanted . . .'

Well, there has always been a proportion of kids who aspired to nothing more than a steady job with a pay packet on Friday nights. There's evidence to suggest that as that possibility has receded they have simply given up thinking about it. They'll worry about it when the school-gate clangs behind them for the last time, no sooner. And they won't get depressed about it, in the way mature unemployed people do, till much later. Probably the most worrying symptom I saw among teenagers was the acceptance of the idea of life without work.

Rather like the bomb, it came into the category of things you were powerless to prevent, and must therefore put out of your mind. And you're never alone on the dole. Your mates are in the same boat. You cut off contact with those who aren't.

One young man, 18 and old enough to have started feeling the pain and boredom of unemployment, explained it like this;

'You can't keep expecting your mates who are in work to buy you drinks so you stop going round with them. You can't take a girl out with no money to pay for her. So you spend your time hanging around the city centre with other unemployed lads. If there's trouble with another gang, well, a bit of aggro relieves the boredom. I can take it now. I don't think I'll be able to take it in 5 years' time.'

'What worries me,' said the mother of the 18-year-old girl mentioned previously, 'is what they'll be like as adults – if they ever become adults in the true sense of being responsible for their own lives. They'll have had no experience of being independent from their parents. I can see us supporting our kids into their middle-age, lumbered with adolescents for life!'

2

Psychological problems

DEPRESSION

Teenagers suffer from depression like the rest of us suffer from the common cold. Depression of the mild, short-lived variety, that is, where they can be plunged into a state of despair by a spot on the chin, hair that won't behave or a boy-friend who fails to telephone.

When depression becomes a dominant mood, however, it may require professional help. There are two common types of serious adolescent depression. The first is a sort of emptiness and lack of feeling that resembles mourning. At least that's how the sufferer interprets it. In fact it may be that he has feelings but they are bottled up because he is unable to accept them or express them.

The second type of depression stems from repeated experience of failure – perhaps at school, at work, in attempts to get work, or in relationships. The last straw – which may prompt a suicide attempt in this type of depression – is the loss of a relationship, with a parent, friend or boy/girl-friend.

SUICIDE

In Britain, seven young people, on average, commit suicide each week. After road accidents, it is the most common cause of death in this age group. The figures for completed suicides however, are a mere drop in the ocean beside the estimated ones for attempted suicides. In the USA it is suggested that between 200,000 and 400,000 young people attempt suicide annually. Most teenagers, in this country too, will have a friend or acquaintance who has taken an overdose or otherwise tried to end their lives.

Why do they do it?

It is hard for adults to understand why someone with what seems like a bright future and everything to live for would end their life.

The mother of a student who hanged himself, said, 'I wish we'd kept in contact more when he went away to university. I'm sure a lot of parents don't realise their children still need them after they leave home. We still can't belive he would do such a thing. I can't bear the thought of him feeling that life wasn't worth living.'

That particular young man had just come to the end of a long-standing and very close relationship with his first and only girl-friend. The break-up of a romance is a fairly common reason for a suicide attempt. Others include school problems, conflict with parents, rejection by a friend, trouble with the police, pregnancy (real or imagined), fear of illness and the loss of a parent or someone close. Often it is an accumulation of a series of difficulties, topped off by a lack of communication between parent and child, which means that the young person has no-one to turn to for support.

Says Peter Eldrid, Youth Officer of the Samaritans (which clocks up 80,000 calls annually from people under 25, 25,000 of these under 16): 'Very often young people have all the materially and socially acceptable things in their lives but that doesn't make any difference. In the main, relationships are what matter in life, and even if people have social problems which make life difficult, they can usually cope if they have people they can talk to. Feeling loved and believing that you are important as an individual is vital.'

More girls attempt suicide, but of the boys who attempt it, more succeed. The teenage girl who over-doses on whatever pills happen to be handy, is a regular occurrence in every doctor's and social worker's life. They probably do not mean to kill themselves. They are making a desperate cry for help. Nobody knows how many of these cries go tragically wrong and the girl dies. All suicide attempts, and all talk of suicide by teenagers should be taken seriously.

Dr Edna Irwin, psychiatrist and head of a hospital Adolescent Unit, says: 'A lot of girls who attempt suicide are driven by anger. "I'll show them. They'll be sorry when I'm dead," is how the reasoning goes.

'If you are 14 and your boy-friend tells you he doesn't want to see you again, and you ring your mother at work for comfort, but she tells you she can't talk now, you might just turn to the aspirin bottle for consolation.

'With a young girl, if I cannot find any other reason for an overdose, I will look for a sexual reason. Incest, a relationship with a friend of the family that she daren't let anyone else know about – or with mother's new husband or boyfriend. The overdose is a way out in such situations. They cannot tell anyone, but if they are taken into hospital, they reason, they will *have* to tell the staff there. Nobody can blame them, when they are lying at death's door.'

As always, when the suicide attempt is successful, parents are left with the agony, the guilt and the same old question – 'Where did we go wrong?'

Said Margaret, whose daughter killed herself under the wheels of an underground train: 'I've thought thousands of times: "What did I say wrong, didn't she realise we loved her?"'

3

Anorexia Nervosa – a disease for our time?

Jane is 15 years old, with gigantic dark eyes in a gaunt face, and matchstick legs encased in woollen tights to keep out the cold, though it's mid-summer. It is her second visit to the Anorexic Aid meeting. The idea of this chain of self-help groups is for anorexia and bulimia sufferers to get together and share their experiences and worries. Jane, however, says little, though she is an intelligent girl. Her articulate and informed mother, who persuaded her to come along, does most of her talking for her.

Mother and daughter are aware of this. Jane has regressed from being a typically independent, opinionated teenager into a helpless little girl, afraid to go anywhere without her mother. The effort to collect her thoughts and express her opinions has become frightening and exhausting for her.

Jane cannot understand why this has happened to her, and she desperately wants to be normal again. Unlike the other women in the group she does not accept the label 'anorexic'. She feels it does not apply to her. The others admit to feeling 'fear' of food and sheer terror at stepping on their scales (though they do so several times daily) in case their weight has gone up.

Jane feels the same scale-phobia – but in case her weight has gone down and she'll be back in hospital.

When her weight dropped to just over 5 stone, she was whisked into hospital where she was kept in bed and made to eat 'enormous meals, the kind I couldn't even have faced when I was really well'.

She ate them because only when she had reached a set weight, acceptable on her 5′ 4″ frame, would she be allowed out. 'I was so unhappy,' she says. 'When my parents visited me, I used to cry all the way through visiting time and beg them to take me home. I hated everything about the place. The doctor used to point me out to people as "my anorexic".

'I don't accept I have anorexia. When I hear the others talk, well, I don't feel like that. I didn't want to get slim. I never tried to diet. I just can't bear to eat and I feel tired and ill.'

The doctors however are generally in agreement that Jane is anorexic, or at least suffering from an eating disorder. Her first symptoms were slight weight loss and erratic periods. The latter were put down to being a young girl whose cycle had not yet settled.

'But,' says Jane's mother, 'Jane started her periods early and they had been regular for years.'

Menstruation stopped. Jane's inability to eat grew worse; her health deteriorated and she became fretful and depressed. Finally as the weight loss continued, she was taken into hospital. Now she is out, still seriously underweight, and seeing a psychiatrist regularly: one who has not yet called her 'his anorexic', so she is hopeful that he may unravel the cause of her illness.

She talks about the incidents that immediately preceded the onset. Her best friend moved to the other side of town. A boy she was friendly with ('Not a boy-friend') also moved away. A series of obscene phone calls to the house worried her. School work was a bit of a headache. 'Nothing really dramatic,' she says.

It is, Jane's mother admits, extremely frustrating living with someone who plays with their food rather than eat it and who says she wants to put on weight but refuses to eat. 'My husband loses patience sometimes; it's hard for him to understand and you feel so helpless about her. It does cause a lot of strain on all of us. Sometimes I feel like cheating and giving her a drink made with whole milk when she insists on skimmed, but I don't want to lose her trust. 'You have to play along, however ridiculous it seems.'

Jane's biggest worry is the strain she is inflicting on her family (she has an older brother). 'I don't know why they put up with me,' she says, and her mother gives her a hug.

ANOREXIA – WHO SUFFERS?

Perhaps it's inevitable that a society as concerned as ours with staying slim, should be plagued with a condition known as the slimmers' disease. And that young girls, so conscious of image and plagued with insecurities, would be the chief sufferers.

But anorexia nervosa has been around a long time. In the seventeenth century, it was described by physicians as 'nervous consumption, stemming from sad and anxious cares'.

Nowadays we are not so sure what it stems from. But, as over 90 per cent of teenage girls are estimated to be on a diet at any given time, and only 7 per cent of sufferers are male, social pressures to be the right shape must be a major factor. A lot of girls start off dieting to control their weight, and eventually find that they cannot control their dieting.

But there are other reasons. Many doctors see the condition as a subconscious effort by a young girl to postpone sexual maturity and to hang on to perpetual childhood. Growing up can be frightening, especially if you do it very early.

Many of the girls who suffer from anorexia are early developers who feel ill at ease with their womanly body among their still-childlike friends. Maybe they are subject to advances from older boys which frighten them.

By refusing food, they can solve the problem. They can revert back to their pre-pubescent shape. When their weight reaches a certain point, they lose their periods. Even before the weight loss is dramatic, some emotional mechanism may cause menstruation to cease.

Psychiatrist Dr George Cohen has a mental picture of the typical anorexic, though he is careful to point out that there are plenty of exceptions. She is a teenage girl of above average intelligence, who reached puberty early, and comes from a rather 'proper' family.

'The family may seem very affectionate. They may be highly articulate and communicate well on a surface level. But it's the sort of family in which unpleasantness and arguments and any expression of negative feeling is frowned on. They don't really talk.

'She may be the sort of girl who sees life as something that happens to her, rather than something she controls. The parents are often successful and forceful people, and she may feel that they allow her no say in her own life. When she finds something that she can control, her own weight, she is reluctant to let go of the power.'

An anorexic will go to great lengths to persuade everyone around her that she is eating, whilst managing to hide food or throw it away. She may want to be helped, but not if it means putting on weight. Some girls will hide their ever-diminishing bodies under increasingly large clothes. The most peculiar off-shoot of the condition, for anyone with no personal experience of it, is the total inability to see themselves as others see them.

Tests have shown that a girl suffering from anorexia actually sees her body as larger and fatter than it is – though, oddly, she sees other people at their correct size. Hence the patient Dr Cohen treats, whose size 8 jeans are hanging loosely on her, and who insists that she is grossly overweight. 'If I told you about a friend who finds size 8 clothes too big, what shape would you imagine she was?' he asked her. 'I'd think she was thin,' she answered, 'but I can see I'm fat.' It is almost an hallucination.

There are, Dr Cohen points out, possible 'perks' to being anorexic. You are singled out from the crowd and people treat you gently and don't expect too much of you.' It's a perk that carries a heavy penalty, as one in twenty anorexia patients die from the condition.

On the other hand, you can recover completely, without any permanent effects, and the majority do. For others it will be a life-long battle between normality and the occasional crisis that can trigger off a relapse. Treatments include admittance to hospital, referral to a psychiatrist, psychologist, psychotherapist or counsellor as an out-patient, involving the whole family in family therapy, and joining one of the self-help groups under the umbrella of Anorexic Aid.

They can all provide a measure of help, but everyone concerned agrees that the only person who can really cure an anorexic is herself. She has to want to be cured or no treatment will work.

BULIMIA – THE FLIPSIDE OF ANOREXIA

There is an awful logic about bulimia, a way of having your cake and not eating it. Like an anorexic, a bulimia-sufferer (typically female and in the late teens or early twenties) is obsessed with food and dieting. Unlike an anorexic, however, her desire for food overcomes her determination not to eat.

So you get a vicious circle. She alternately starves, binges and then immediately purges with self-induced vomiting and massive doses of laxatives – 30 or 40 tablets at a time.

Despite this masochistic regime, her body does absorb food, so she is not emaciated and the condition is harder to detect. A third of bulimics have 'graduated' from anorexia. The condition can have far-reaching effects, ranging from bowel and kidney damage to severe psychological problems. Anorexic Aid offers its help and support to bulimia sufferers too.

4

Teenagers and alcohol

There are relatively few teenagers being treated for drink problems. Not because teenagers don't drink too much, unfortunately, but because it takes time to admit – to yourself – that you need help. Until that point, help is impossible, and by the time most people make the admission, they are already out of their teens.

Teenagers are drinking more and earlier. The National Children's Bureau discovered that drinking is more common than smoking among 16-year-olds. Putting the question: 'How long is it since you had an alcoholic drink?' to 12,000 16-year-olds, they found that the answer for 46 per cent was; 'Less than a week ago'. A further 19 per cent had been drinking in the previous month and only 7 per cent had never tasted alcohol.

More than half of all young people first try drink at home . . . the safest place to learn about the effects, according to Josef Ruzek of the Drinkwatchers organisation. 'Too many kids start drinking with their friends on the sly so there are no sensible controls on them at the time they are forming their drinking habits. They develop their social skills under the influence of alcohol and then don't know how to handle situations when they are not drinking. They get into alcohol so early that they never learn to deal properly with the pressures of life.'

So what can parents do to help a son or daughter they suspect is having problems with drink? Keith Chadwick of Aquarius, another counselling group, suggests being alert for the danger signs – mood changes and irritability tied to the drinking pattern, insomnia, poor appetite, or a craving for sweet things and eating enormous amounts between drinking bouts.

'If drink has become the most important thing in a teenager's life and they are sacrificing other pleasures like records and clothes, parents should take it seriously. If a row sends them off for a drink, or they need one before going to a party, they are using it as a prop. That's dangerous. But the hardest part is getting *them* to recognise it. You cannot treat someone for a problem till they acknowledge they have it.'

Kevin:

'An alcoholic' is not a label he cares for. He prefers to say he has a drink problem; a problem that started when he was only 14 years old. He didn't recognise it as such then. It wasn't until a few months ago that Kevin admitted to himself that he was in trouble. By then he was just out of his teens.

Kevin grew up in a multi-racial Inner-city area. His background is mixed race; his father is Pakistani, his mother Irish. The ethnic mix has left him with dark brown eyes and what could pass for an all-year-round suntan, but there are other effects and they are more than skin-deep.

Rightly or wrongly, Kevin traces his problems with drink back to his father's attitude towards him – an attitude he interpreted as disinterest and disappointment.

He's a personable young man, proud of working his way up to a responsible job as head barman in a busy pub. He was on sick leave when I met him, slowly facing up to the realisation that he would never be able to return to his job. Or any other job that gave him easy access to alcohol. This is Kevin's story:

'At school I was very good at sports, particularly football. Lived for it, you might say, at around 14. This local works team asked me to play with them. They were young lads, 18 or 19 mostly. I was big for my age, mature. I fitted in easily with them. Nobody felt I was a kid.

'After a match we'd go down the pub for a few pints. They knew I wasn't earning, so they'd automatically buy my drinks. I suppose they were too young themselves to think of any dangers – or even that they were breaking the law. A man in his thirties or forties might have thought twice.

'It never occurred to my Mom at that stage that I was drinking. She doesn't drink herself. If you don't you're sort of innocent. You don't know what to look out for. My old man didn't seem to notice but then he never noticed anything I did, not till it was too late. If he had, it might have been different.

'We have no relationship at all now, not so you'd notice. The funny thing is I still want him to be pleased with me, to say something nice. It's always been like that. I don't like him, but I suppose I love him. He's my father.'

Kevin has sisters and an older half-brother, his father's son, who lives with the family. 'My half-brother is hard-working, highly-qualified and a practising Muslim. In my father's eyes he's perfect and I'm a very poor comparison.

'I've got a few O-levels, but nobody seemed very interested, so I left school and got a job in a warehouse. The only thing I shone at –

ever – was football. My father never came to see me play. It's not the sort of thing that impresses him.

'I started drinking, I suppose, because I could go to the pub with mates who appreciated my ability, and it was the one place I didn't feel lonely. I didn't turn into a heavy drinker overnight. For one thing I couldn't afford to. It happened gradually and I built up a tolerance that most young lads don't come near. If I'd overdone it at an early age, made myself violently sick or had a few bad hangovers, it might have put me off.

'At work I'd go over the road for a drink at lunch-time. After work there would always be someone around asking if you were coming for a pint. When you're drinking, you've always got mates. When you stop you realise how few friends you really have.'

Perhaps the most surprising thing is how easy Kevin found it to obtain drink at the tender age of 14. It is unusually young, he agrees, but insists that you'll find 16-year-olds propping up any bar.

'You can recognise them even if they look older. They are a bit nervous and unsure of themselves. The barmen can recognise them. Believe me it's far too easy for young kids to buy alcohol. Parents either don't know or don't care.'

At 17, still officially too young to drink in a pub, Kevin was working part-time behind the bar. When a football injury made warehouse work difficult, the job became full-time.

'Great, eh? Just what I needed! When I wasn't behind the bar I was on the other side of it, drinking. Everybody's friend! Then I discovered women – and things started to go wrong. I really fell for this girl, my first serious girl-friend. When we had a row and she broke off the relationship, I went into my self-destruct routine. I drank myself insensible, took an overdose and ended up having my stomach pumped out in hospital.

'That's what I'm told happened. I don't remember anything between starting to drink and waking up in hospital. It was the usual cry for help. If I had been really planning to kill myself. I wouldn't have dragged myself round to the pub to tell them I'd swallowed the pills, would I? They got me to hospital.

'In the hospital they wanted to know why I'd made a suicide attempt, before releasing me. All I would say was "I had my reasons. It's my business". So they let me go. I didn't tell anyone why I'd done it, even my family. Why? I just felt it was personal – maybe I felt it was a bloody stupid thing to do over a girl.

'You see, I could never talk about anything like that at home, about feelings. If I'd gone home and said to my mother, "I've met this girl. I think I'm in love with her," her reaction would have been one of two things. Either "Don't be so bloody daft" or "Have you got some girl into trouble?"

'It's fairly common for parents to think the worst of teenagers. Maybe it's different in middle-class homes, but I doubt it. You might only have ever said hello to the girl at the bus-stop, but your parents will assume there is sexual activity involved. They never give teenagers credit for deep feelings, for any sensitivity. They laugh or they reduce it to something sordid, at least round my way they do.

'That's not to say that my old lady doesn't care about me. She does, I know. But never, since I was about 12 or 13, have I been able to spend ten minutes in her company without a row starting.

'It's hard to say what we row about – everything and anything. We just don't seem to be able to talk without yelling at each other. She hints instead of coming right out with things. When it first got through to her that I was drinking a lot, she would never confront me with it or tell me to stop. She would give digs, make sly remarks.

'Whenever a row starts in our house it always ends up with me the centre of the argument. It's hard to explain. If my young sister stands in front of the television while everyone else is trying to watch, they'll get annoyed with her first. But if I open my mouth to tell her to move, suddenly the whole weight of the aggro shifts to me. Suddenly I'm the centre of the problem. It happens all the time. I don't think I'm imagining that I'm the scapegoat for the family's arguments. It's happened since I was a kid and it still happens now when I go home.'

The saga of Kevin's drinking from this point is familiar to anyone involved with alcohol abuse. Soon he was drinking fifteen pints a day, creeping up to 16½ stones in weight, too overweight and lethargic to play football. There was the party of where he remembered nothing beyond greeting the first guests. Still his work was not affected; in fact he was promoted.

There was another troubled romance, which precipitated a solitary ten-day drinking bout, otherwise known as a holiday in Ireland. 'When I got back I found my girl-friend shacked up with my best mate. Self-destruct time again. I began to drink even more. I couldn't sleep. I was sick first thing in the morning and couldn't start the day without a drink. I wasn't eating or washing. I was living out of carrier-bags, falling down. One night I couldn't stand up behind the bar. Another day I vomited blood.

'Eventually I went to the doctor. She told me I had slight liver damage. She asked if I drank a lot. I said, no, not a lot. I honestly didn't believe 15 pints was a lot. You lose all sense of proportion when you are only moving among other people who drink heavily.

'For 9 weeks, I didn't drink at all. I saved enough to put a deposit on one of those singles' flatlets, where I now live. I couldn't go on living with the family. I felt ashamed. The problem was that to avoid alcohol, I cut myself off from everyone. I didn't go out except to work, then straight home. Ridiculous really – the loneliness got so bad that I started drinking to ease it. Alone this time, and at home.'

When his mother visited and found him drunk and unwashed, amid the ever-increasing dust and dirty dishes, there was a show-down. For the first time, she took a firm line. She threatened never to see him again, unless he sought help with his drink problem.

'I went along with it,' he says, 'I let her find a clinic and make an appointment. Not because I had a problem, you understand. I still didn't believe I had. I was doing it to please my mother and because I was so low and suicidal I had no will left.

'The first time I saw a counsellor at the Aquarius centre for problem drinkers, I was so nervous I couldn't speak. I shot out of the chair, straight into the nearest pub for a drink to steady my nerves. The second time I went, I had a drink before going in. It wasn't the way to do it I know, but at least it gave me the courage to admit I had a problem. That's the first hurdle.

'The first fortnight – I'd signed a contract not to drink for two weeks – was the hardest of my life. I had to get time off work. I found I couldn't pass a pub without going in. In the end, I took to going out without any money, but you still meet mates who want to buy you a drink. It's hard to change your whole way of life. I was very agitated, got myself worked up for nothing.

'Then Aquarius held a party with no drinks served. That was a real eye-opener. I stayed sober and enjoyed myself at a social function for the first time since I was in my early teens.

'Now I understand why I drank – because I was lonely, because it was an occupational hazard, because I enjoyed it and it calmed me down when I was under pressure. I've learned that I have to accept responsibility for my own drinking. I may get pie-eyed because a girl lets me down, but it's not her fault.

'I live on my own, but I go home quite a bit. My mother, as long as we don't spend too long together, is great; really proud that I'm sticking to the régime. My sisters are understanding too. My half-brother makes it clear he thinks alcoholics should be shut away and my old man just ignores it. He didn't expect anything better of me anyway.

'I wish they hadn't let my drinking get so far out of hand before forcing a showdown. Parents seem to be afraid to confront you with their suspicions. I mean they don't talk *to* you when you are in your teens, they talk *at* you. Or they ignore you for years; then they try to lay down the law and it's too late.

'The real problem is that drink is too readily available to kids. If you know where to look – and you soon learn – you can drink from six in the morning to midnight. Pubs are the only places for young lads to go. There's nothing else to do in the evenings, especially at that really vulnerable period between 16 and 18. That's when most of them start to drink heavily. Parents shouldn't just assume that they'll grow out of it, that they'll be okay. A lot won't. I wasn't.'

Anne:
'I have to make sure that every access to drink is locked. You daren't leave money lying around. I say to my daughter, Donna, "Watch your purse." It's terrible to have to admit that your son is stealing from you. But Jim has robbed us, and he will do it again, given the chance, because he has a disease.'

The disease is alcoholism. Anne, a small, pretty woman in her 40s, clearly finds it easier to accept her 18-year-old son's problems if she sees them in that light. Jim steadfastly refuses to admit he has a problem. 'What can you do?' she asks, wringing her hands.

Anne has been attending the local Al-Anon Family Group, for relatives of alcoholics, just to have people to talk to. They have tried to keep it from the regulars at the pub she and her husband run. It doesn't do to take your problems into work.

It started she thinks when Jim was 14. Anne was divorced. When she married Bernard, they moved to a different area, as landlords of a public house.

Jim, 'a shy lad, lacking in confidence', missed his old familiar friends. To keep him busy and in pocket money, they gave him a little job 'bottling up', placing bottles on the shelves. Occasionally and worryingly, a bottle would disappear, first of beer, later of spirits. Jim acted mystified, then one day, they found him drunk with a half-empty bottle of vodka.

He ran out of the house, fell down and injured himself and ended up in hospital. 'He was violent and abusive,' said Anne, 'not at all like my boy'.

Anne was shaken, but convinced herself that Jim, like many a lad before him, had learned his lesson. Life went back to normal. The matter was forgotton. When his birthday came round, a party was organised as usual. 'People brought bottles. There was drink,' Anne said. 'Teenagers expect it.'

But for Jim it was the start of the alcoholic merry-go-round again. Afterwards, drink started disappearing again, money too. Everything had to be locked up. The family got a move – back to the district where Jim had grown up, to another pub. Anne was full of hope.

'I thought he'd meet up with his old friends and forget about the drink. He was really looking forward to it. But things had changed. Houses had been knocked down, and a lot of his old mates had moved or found new friends. "They've deffed me out, Mum", he told me.'

By this time, Jim had left school. His dole money, after giving his mother a few pounds for his keep, went on alcohol. On one occasion his sister confronted him with six vodka bottles found under his bed. He denied all knowledge of them.

'In front of us he drank Coca-Cola,' Anne says. 'I tasted it once and found it laced with vodka, but he just denied everything. You began to wonder if it was you or him who was mad.

'Once, when I confronted him with empty bottles and demanded an explanation, he lost his temper and started to smash the room up. He'd have hit me only Bernard hit him first. That's something my husband has never done to my kids. He used to get on well with both of them. It was Jim who first suggested we should get married.

'It shook us, me and Bernard. It's come between us. Now we rarely mention the subject of drink. There's virtually no communication in the house. We're both frightened of saying the wrong thing.

'His drinking goes in bouts. He'll be okay for weeks and you start to hope. I've just had my hopes dashed this morning; that's why I'm so jittery now. Things have been going well for a long time. I've got Jim involved with the pub darts team – anything to relieve the boredom of unemployment, which I think has a lot to do with his drinking. He's got to know other lads his age. I was saying to Bernard just last week, "I think he's growing up, growing out of depending on alcohol."

'Then this morning, his dole day, I got him up early and he set off to pick up his money and see if there was a job doing. The next I saw of him was after lunch. My heart sank. It was plain he'd been drinking. It was in his walk and the glassy stare.

'When I called him over, he stood a good distance from me. He thinks if you can't smell the drink you don't know. I asked if he'd been drinking and he was very insulted. He was so adamant, I did wonder for a minute if I was imagining it. Then he launched into this story about how he'd nearly landed this job as a plumber. I didn't know whether to laugh or cry. He couldn't change a washer on a tap. He makes up these stories when he's been drinking, to stop you asking questions or to give himself an alibi.

'The other thing he does is get very helpful. I suppose it's the guilt. He'll dust and polish the house. I found he'd washed up and made all the sandwiches for the bar this evening. Oh, he's a good lad really. If he wasn't so likeable I'd have washed my hands of him. I've often felt like it. I've been tempted to ring up his father and say, "You deal with him. He's your son."'

'It's Bernard who talks me out of it. I don't think Bernard wants to admit he has failed, that we both have. Bernard feels bitter towards Jim now – well he has stolen hundreds of pounds from him through the business. 'There's a limit to how many chances you can give someone, how long you can go on caring.'

5

Drug abuse – the ultimate nightmare

Drugs are every parent's nightmare. 'I don't care what my kids do, as long as they are not sticking needles in their arms,' said one mother: a sentiment echoed by many others.

The fears, fuelled by newspaper reports of deaths from glue-sniffing and cheap heroin available to teenagers at a few pounds a 'fix', are not unjustified. What is unjustified – or so it seems to young people – is parental panic. The kind of panic which causes parents to accuse them, wrongly, of 'sniffing' because they have read that there is a local epidemic; or to ban them from parties because they have heard that cannabis is sometimes smoked at these.

'You'd think after 17 years my parents would know me,' said one aggrieved girl from a council estate, where glue-sniffing was rife. 'I have a mind of my own and I'm not going to be led astray by some snotty-nosed kid with a glue bag.'

'My mother once asked me if I'd ever been to a party where there was cannabis,' said a 17-year-old boy. 'I didn't know what to say. I've hardly ever been to a party where at some point someone wasn't smoking pot. It doesn't mean you have to join in – or that if you do, you will be a pot-head for life. I tried it once and it just made me feel dizzy. End of interest. I was just experimenting.'

'You can't tell parents because they think all drugs are the same – terminal,' he added, getting closer to one of the villains of the piece, ignorance. 'Parents don't know a lot about drugs, do they?'

It would be grossly presumptuous to agree with him, and yet . . . Many parents did a bit of experimenting with the so-called 'soft' drugs in their own youth, in the laid-back Sixties. They talk from experience – and probably with a bias. Those who didn't experiment absorbed a fair amount of information from the media – and with it a number of myths. And that leaves a hefty number who only read sensational headlines or glean their information from what the next-door neighbour says his aunt heard on telly last weekend. All-in-all, a lot of parents *don't* know a lot of facts about drug abuse and compensate with a lot of strong, but not necessarily rational, gut feelings. Those forced to find out often do so at the bitterly painful moment when their own child's involvement is staring them in the face.

Joan Goode, of Drugline, a counselling service for people with a drug problem and their families or friends, has one cardinal rule for parents concerned that their children may be experimenting with drugs of any kind. 'You must talk to them – and you must know what you are talking about. Find out all the facts as we know them, about all drugs.'

'Give them the facts, tell them about the dangers, but not a totally unrealistic shock-horror story. Don't lie to them. Cannabis, for instance, is not physically addictive, so don't say it is. It is something that teenagers tend to dabble in because their friends are trying it. They usually grow out of it. Heroin is a different matter. It can be a killer and they must know it. But even here, telling a 15-year-old that he may be dead by 30 if he takes heroin has little effect. Thirty is a lifetime away, after all. It's old age.

'The heavy-handed attitude doesn't work. Don't lock them in their room and refuse to let them out. It only gives them something else to kick against – and besides, you have to open the door sooner or later. Better to emphasise the fact that you are honestly worried and get them interested in the idea of a contract, where they play a major part in defining the terms.

'The idea is that they give up glue or cannabis in return for some provision on your side. I am not really talking here about someone who is addicted to heroin but parents should not see that as hopeless either. Many, many young people have proved that you can come off – and stay off – heroin with medical help and the support of family and an organisation like ours.'

The Institute for the Study of Drug Dependence (see address on p. 179) issues some excellent literature which will tell you anything you ever wanted to know about drugs, but didn't know where to ask. It describes the form the various drugs take, the effects, the particular dangers and treatments. Everything is covered – from solvents, through pills, cannabis, hallucinogenics (LSD, 'magic' mushrooms) to the opiates, like heroin.

Nowadays, cannabis is probably the most widely used. Hardly a week passes without some jet-setter or pop-star being arrested for carrying it. It is one of the so-called 'soft' drugs; no more dangerous than alcohol and a lot less dangerous than cigarettes say its supporters, who want it legalised.

It is not physically addictive like the opiates, but a query remains over whether it may be the thin end of the wedge, a first step on the ladder to the harder stuff. It may well introduce young people to the drug scene and bring them into contact with sources of other drugs.

Heroin can be – and often is – a killer. It used to be mainly injected and very expensive, which meant at least that it was outside the scope of younger teenagers. Lately, however, an influx of cheap heroin has flooded the market, making it accessible to schoolchildren, who turn to petty theft to finance the habit.

The younger heroin-users tend to 'sniff', rather than inject the powder. Often it is placed on a piece of foil, heated from underneath with a match, and the resultant droplets chased and sniffed through a straw. Hence the picturesque name of this new deadly game – 'Chasing the dragon.' The habit is reputedly endemic on the poorer housing estates in major cities, and increasing elsewhere.

The increased numbers have put a massive strain on the limited number of National Health hospital clinics, set up to help drug mis-users in the 1960s. Before the increase in young addicts, the facilities were already hopelessly inadequate. providing no more than a couple of hundred beds, countrywide, where people could be gradually, painlessly weaned off heroin.

The whole medical model of treatment for addicts has been questioned in any case since so many people go back on drugs as soon as they leave the clinic. It is partly because of this that self-help groups have flourished, some started by parents. Many are now funded on a shoe-string by the government, which knows a useful service when it spots one.

The groups can usually offer an informed and understanding volunteer ear at the end of a telephone, and a face-to-face counselling service for drug mis-users and/or their families. Some, like Families Anonymous (the twin of Addicts Anonymous) run regular meetings where parents can get together to thrash out their feelings and support each other.

'You feel as if you are the only parents in the world who have ever been through this experience and you are riddled with guilt,' explained one mother whose teenage son is a heroin addict. 'Just talking to other parents takes away some of that irrational guilt and gives you the strength to keep trying to get your child back to normal, however hopeless it seems at times.' Sally, whose daughter Wendy was an addict for six years, knows all about such feelings.

Sally, mother of Wendy, an ex-heroin addict:
Sally is co-founder of one of the support organisations for drug addicts and their families which have sprung up around the country. She started it 'to try and prevent other families having to go through what we went through in the past six years. This is the length of time Sally's daughter, Wendy has been registered as a heroin addict, though her introduction to drugs came earlier, in her mid-teens. Here is Sally's story.

'She came home one day unexpectedly. She looked terrible: grey, nervous and she'd really lost weight. She said: "I have something to tell you, but I want us to sit back to back like book-ends because I don't want to see your face when you hear." So we sat down and she said, "I'm a heroin addict, Mum – will you help me?"'

'When you look back, the question is always why, what went wrong, what did I do wrong? It's the one all parents ask when their child turns to drugs – and the one nobody can answer. Wendy was never a very easy, happy child from her early teens. Her brother is considerably older than her. We moved around a lot as a family so maybe she lacked stability, maybe she was lonely.

'Certainly she was insecure and jealous. She would say to me, "You love Dad more than me, don't you?" When she was about fourteen, I was in hospital and she and my husband visited me. I didn't take much notice of the seating arrangements, I was just glad to have them. Afterwards she brought up the fact that her father sat closest to me, between us, and she had to sit on a chair further away.

'On another occasion she said to me out of the blue "I can't be like you". Well, I didn't see any particular reason why she should be like me and told her so. "But people like you and they don't like me", she said. Wendy is adopted and I sometimes wondered if it was something to do with this, some sort of identity crisis. I've told her all I know about her mother, which is very little. She is in New Zealand now, where she came from.

'The upshoot of it all, however, was that in her mid-teens Wendy was a difficult girl. Her behaviour, I felt, was more than the normal teenage rebellion, but when I tried to talk to people including my GP, they acted as if I was exaggerating. The inference was that all teenagers are difficult and I was being a bit silly.

'Still at school, she started to go out with her first boy-friend, and she became pregnant. Something else I regret is that Wendy went to an all-girls school. When they grow up surrounded by boys in a mixed school they can take them or leave them. Mixing only with girls, they become very silly about boys and liable to throw themselves into the arms of the first one who comes along.

'Very early on, she told me she thought she was pregnant – and soon afterwards, she began a natural miscarriage. Again, when we saw the doctor I tried to tell him how worried I was about Wendy and he laughed. He said I should be thankful we had a good enough relationship for her to confide in me – he saw girls eight months pregnant who hadn't broken the news to their parents.

'Then came the next boy-friend. It was with him that the drug thing began. She told us about him. "You won't like him," she said, "He's in care." I thought, "Well I'm not going to fall into that trap – making him seem more attractive by disapproving," so we asked her to bring him home. We really did try to get on with him, but it was obvious he was not a good influence.'

The boy-friend, Sally believes, introduced her daughter to cannabis. Sally found out she was taking it by intercepting her letters. There were rows, and in the face of opposition, the romance petered out. But Wendy remained difficult.

'She criticised our way of life continuously. "I don't like square people like you and your friend," she'd sneer. "I like unusual freaky people." She left school, which she hated, and got a job in a Radiography Department against stiff competition. Proof of what a bright and charming girl she could be. Her social life was involved with a crowd who liked to spend their evenings at a club in the nearest city. Her moods used to swing wildly. In retrospect, she was probably already taking amphetamines.

'At 17, Wendy told us she couldn't stand our middle-class dump a minute longer. She was going to share a bed-sit in the city with another girl. We had two choices – reject her or support her. She left with our blessings. I kept telling myself she was just trying to find her identity, she'd be fine.

'The idea was she'd commute to her job, but it was a long way off, and she soon gave it up. I thought she'd have to come home then, but no, she just went on to Social Security. She even moved to a bigger flat on state support. Honestly, they talk about parental responsibility, but the state just takes them over.

'We saw Wendy occasionally. She didn't look at all well, but she wouldn't tell me what was wrong – till that day when she came home to confess and ask for help. You know, after all the clues and my suspicions, I still couldn't take it in. I wondered for a moment if she was fantasising, making it up. But she was serious. She had to get to a doctor, she said, because soon she was going to be very poorly indeed with withdrawal symptoms.

'My doctor didn't want to know. He suggested we contact the nearest addiction unit, the only one outside London at the time.

'Wendy was just 18 and the unit made it pretty clear to me that I was to have no involvement. They would take Wendy on, if she showed she was motivated; that she wanted to be cured, not just that I wanted it. She was in for six weeks. The communication with us, her family, during that time was almost non-existent. The consultant would never see us because, we were told, he was a very busy man.

'However, her current boy-friend had turned up, and the people at the unit seemed happy that Wendy should live with him when she came out, though not in the area they had been in. It was felt that drugs were too easily available there. There was no recognition that this was not only a medical problem but a family problem; that after their treatment is over, the family are the ones left to pick up the pieces.

'My husband and I also had to undergo what is known as a social enquiry. This involved a social worker questioning us on Wendy's background back to the year dot. It includes such irrelevant classics as how I potty-trained her and whether she had friends in as a small child. All it achieved was to increase our guilt, which was already sky high. It made us feel that Wendy's drug addiction was definitely the result of something we had done – or failed to do – in her childhood.

'The one concession I had got them to make at the hospital was that they would tell me if Wendy walked out and that's exactly what she did. She discharged herself. She had a £10 giro cheque on her. That was cashed at the first post-office and used to buy drugs. She had, of course, taken care to bring a needle out of the hospital to inject herself.

'It was at that stage that we learned the first, hard lesson. In a controlled environment, like hospital, where they can wean addicts gradually, it is quite easy to come off drugs. Staying off them is the problem. We actually believed it was a onc-off spell, that Wendy would be completely cured and back to the girl she was before her first shot. She wasn't – she never will be. It was just the start, the first step on the merry-go-round.'

Wendy's roundabout has been crowded with painful stops and starts. In times of greatest need, she always comes home. When she was at a very low ebb, mentally and physically, Sally found a community for addicts in Oxfordshire, the Ley Community.

She was supposed to stay for 18 months – the later part of the stay spent working outside the community and leading a more or less normal life.

'Wendy almost made it, but after 15 months she announced that she was leaving with Gavin, the boy-friend she had met in the Community. I pleaded, but she assured me she was okay. They had already learned everything they could in the place. But soon she was on drugs again – they both were. They came to live with us. Oh, it was ghastly. They were in a terrible state. It's so hard to live with someone on drugs. You daren't ever let them get their hands on money, because you know exactly how they will spend it. One day they set off for Oxford, where Gavin had to attend a court hearing. They stayed on the train. The next we heard they were in London.

'In London, Wendy went to see one of these independent Doctors of Addiction and began paying her £80 a week for a heroin substitute. She would then sell half the drugs to be able to afford the next lot and to live. It's perfectly legal for these doctors to prescribe privately, but surely they know what's going on? It was obvious, with Wendy on the dole and the way she dressed and looked, that she couldn't have found £80 a week; that she must be selling it. But there were apparently no questions asked.'

The sorry story goes on. Soon Gavin was in prison for pushing drugs and Wendy sick and anorexic, asked once more to come home. 'For a moment we thought of saying no. How much can a family take? But she did come home and again Sally helped get her into the addiction unit she had been in years before.

'They got her off all right, but it was a much harder job this time. I think she was out of her head when she came off. She was very, very distressed. She kept saying she hated herself, that she could not live with the guilt or the pain she had caused us. "If ever I go back on drugs again, it will be my last time. I'll finish it," she told us.'

She very nearly did. Wendy injected herself with a lethal dose. But before she died she was found. 'When the medics told me that they had brought her round, my first reaction was, "Oh I wish you hadn't." I'd never imagined it possible to feel like that about your own child, but I just didn't feel we could take any more, as a family. How could I face what I believed was inevitable – watching her kill herself either by accident or design? I'd had enough.'

And so, after the next relapse – when Wendy was back home and again smuggling drugs into the house – her mother threw her out. Incredibly, Wendy, on her own, pulled herself up from the depths. When she next rang her mother – and was asked to come home – she was off drugs.

She is now home, over two stone heavier and free of drugs. Sally has the caution born of bitter experience. 'It's early days. I'm constantly aware that anything can trigger her off again. She is not the same girl she was. She finds it hard to concentrate, but she is trying hard.

'We count our blessings. So many of the young people I have met on the drug scene over the years are dead. I am beginning to believe that if you survive long enough, you can grow out of heroin addiction. That at least is what I'd like to believe.'

Wendy.
'At 17, I was so proud of being a heroin user, I used to roll my sleeves up, so that people would see the tracks on my arms. I'd really get a buzz out of catching them staring or whispering. I'd smile to myself and think "I'm not like you, not one of the sheep. I'm different. I'm special."'

A chat with Wendy, ex-heroin addict, dispels a few myths . . .

that teenagers get on to drugs because they are led astray by bad company or encouraged by pushers; that they do it to escape reality; that they regard it as a shameful secret vice; that youthful addicts come from unhappy, disadvantaged homes.

Wendy is intelligent, articulate and middle-class. She was brought up from babyhood by loving adoptive parents. No, she says, dispelling yet another myth, she has never had any desire to find her biological mother or suffered any identity crisis. Her older brother, also adopted, who has experienced some of these feelings about his 'roots' never went off the tracks as she did.

'I don't believe in the easy answers, the cop-out explanations. For what it's worth, I was a lonely, unhappy child with no friends. I had emotional problems, but so did thousands of other kids and they didn't start using heroin. I don't know why I was friendless, I suspect it was because I was very insecure and to hide this I'd put on a big-headed act and show off and tell lies. People always sussed me out though, and that made me very nasty. I hated being sussed out.

'At that time, we were living in a private house on the edge of a council estate. It was the only big house around and the kids from the estate used to taunt me and call me a snob. To fit in, I would try and get down to the level of the worst of them. Whatever they got up to, I'd try to do the same.

'By the time I was 13, I was smoking dope and taking LSD and speed. My school, though it seemed respectable from the outside, was the sort of place where the teachers were relieved if the cigarette they found you smoking in the playground was only tobacco. Being an all-girls school, we were very keen on boys. Boys were always being smuggled into the grounds or we'd sneak away to meet the older boys at the Tech.

'If you make sure you hang around the right crowd, there will be pot and pills going – and I always picked the right boys. I'd always fix my sights on the one with the longest hair, the tattiest jeans, the worst reputation. These boys weren't leading me astray, whatever my parents believed. I wanted to be involved in the drug scene. My whole life was devoted to being a rebel.

'Later on, when I was hooked on heroin, I felt guilty about letting my parents down and tried to keep it from them. But in my early teens, I didn't care what they thought. I didn't consider that they had feelings – or if I did, I enjoyed shocking them.

'I wouldn't talk to them. I blamed them for everything that went wrong. I believed they expected too much of me and that they were too conventional. If only they had been different I felt, my life would have been so much better. I used to wander around in a world of my own. They bought me a horse, to give me a less damaging interest I suppose. Well, I was interested in my horse, but not in other horses and other people, which is what they hoped would happen. What actually happened was that I spent all my time alone with the horse. I just withdrew further into my own world.'

About the pregnancy, which happened when she was still at school, Wendy says: 'My only friends were older boys, and my only concept of friendship was to give them what they wanted. I'm not proud of it, but that's why I slept around. I had to tell my mother I was pregnant, but I wouldn't let her support me. I remember thinking, "How could she understand? She's never been able to have babies herself." When I lost the baby I locked myself in the bathroom and miscarried alone.

'I really hated straight people, even those my own age. I'd look at them at a party or in a pub, laughing and shouting, and I'd think to myself that they were like a bunch of kids, boring and immature. I felt very superior because they had not had the experiences I had.

'By the time I left school I was determined to try heroin. You might say it was my one ambition, I'd seen people stoned and I'd read about people who took hard drugs. We'd had this film and a talk about drug addiction at school – all about the horrors of it and the number of addicts who die young. It was like a red rag to a bull. It seemed the last word in glamour.'

She couldn't wait to get away from home and head for the big city – to an area with a reputation for the Bohemian lifestyle.

Unerringly too, she sought out a relationship with a known heroin addict, Brian, 8 years older than her.

'I begged him to let me try heroin, but there was no way he would give me any. He thought of me as a sweet innocent little thing. So I got some off his friend instead. That first injection – Wow! I thought, "This is for me!" It was never quite as good again, but from then on, I was using anything I could get my hands on. Brian decided that he had to start supplying me to keep some control over me or I would kill myself.

'It was at this point and only then that I started taking drugs for the traditional reason – to escape reality. I wouldn't worry about a daughter of mine smoking pot; it's a sociable habit, done with other people. But opiates, like heroin, completely isolate you in your own world. It replaces everything. Nothing and no-one matters when you get stoned. It is the ultimate escape.

'It's very easy for a girl to get the money for drugs – all she has to do is whore. The ones who can't face that – and I was one of them – generally latch on to a fellow who has to bring in enough to feed both their habits. It works both ways. A girl can be very useful.

'Most addicts "do" chemists – they break in and steal drugs. The police will immediately look for a known addict with a record, like Brian. So he'd fix himself up with an alibi and send me to break in. When the police arrived, I'd be all sweet and innocent and they didn't have a scrap of evidence to connect me. . . .

'Most blokes wouldn't think twice about sending their girl-friend out on the streets to get the money for a fix. One of the nicest things about Gavin, the man I'm going to marry, is that he'd never ask me to whore.'

Wendy has been in addiction units, presumably to be cured, five times. Each time she walked out of hospital and back into her old ways. Why?

'Because I didn't genuinely want to give up drugs. I went into hospital because I couldn't get any drugs and needed care. I got sick enough to dial 999. Withdrawal symptoms vary in intensity, but they get worse the longer you are a user because your doses are higher. You are in great pain, your skin is crawling, you desperately want to sleep. Eventually you have convulsions. At least the clinics will keep you on a maintenance dose of a heroin substitute, not enough to get high, and avoid the worst.'

The turning point for Wendy came after her last stay in hospital. 'I'd never had such a bad time coming off. Gavin and I had split up. I kept thinking of the suffering I'd caused people, particularly my parents. I didn't want to live.'

She made three attempts at suicide by drug overdose, one of them in the family's bathroom. Her mother, at breaking-point, told her she could no longer have her at home. Wendy tried killing herself under the wheels of a car. 'It stopped in time. I thought "I can't even kill myself to stop my parents suffering."'

She went back to London, but for reasons which neither Wendy nor her mother understand – and don't want to tempt fate by examining too closely – she did not go back to drugs.

Partly it was down to Gavin, back in her life and making his own attempt to break free of heroin. Something else – she had for the first time become frightened of what heroin could do. Not of death ('I've seen so many friends die. What is there to fear?') but of the physical and mental agony of withdrawal and the sordidness of the life.

'I'd stopped thinking I was unique the first time I joined the other addicts in Piccadilly waiting for their prescriptions. But it takes a long time to see how sordid is the criminal life that goes with the habit.'

Wendy is home, doing voluntary work with handicapped people; something she'd like to do as a job. Gavin is living nearby, an out-patient at the local clinic. They plan to marry. 'They say two addicts can never make it together, but I couldn't live with someone who had not been addicted. They just don't understand. Gavin and I can support each other.'

'Looking back I don't see what my parents could have done to stop me experimenting. Perhaps parents shouldn't keep bailing their kids out. Let them hit rock-bottom early, so they can see the reality of an addict's life. I was protected from the worst for quite a while – maybe too long.'

6

Glue sniffing – 'Like being a leper'

I met Keith and Carl at the glue-sniffers' group, run two evenings a week at a Health Centre by Bob, a Health Education Officer. Bob is keen to point out that solvent abuse is not new, to him anyway. In his job, he's been aware since the 1960s that kids were sniffing all manner of substances readily available from supermarkets and chemists.

The purpose of the group is to provide counselling, company, guidance and a limited social outlet to kids who have been banned from clubs and pubs in the area because of their habit. All are boys, though a couple of girls attend once-in-a-while.

The smell of glue hangs heavily in the small room. (How can parents 'not know' their child is sniffing?) It floats up from their breath, clothes and hair – and from the supplies some of them are carrying in their pockets. Indeed, many of them are already high.

Arriving at a glue-sniffing clinic carrying glue seems bizarre; rather like bringing a bottle to an AA meeting. But if it was banned on the premises, many of the boys wouldn't come and there would be no chance for a quiet bit of group counselling. Instead they would be out sniffing, probably in some dangerous spot. Most of them can tell tales of mates who stumbled in front of a car, fell from a height or got into a fight with someone bigger 'under the influence'.

'You get into fights because people treat you like dirt when they know you sniff,' said one boy. 'They take it out on your family too. It's like being a leper.' But he still sniffs.

Some figures suggest that one in three teenagers try glue-sniffing, though all but 10 per cent of these give up after a few trials. Only about 5 per cent become hardened, solitary sniffers, but even those on it for a short while can put their health at risk. 'I try to persuade the lads that nobody *needs* glue,' says Bob. 'But it's a hard job. They have such a bleak future you see.'

Glue sniffing

For glue, read solvent. What the kids sniffing the daubs of glue out of crisp bags are doing is inhaling the vapours of the solvent in the glue, as it evaporates.

Many household products contain solvent, which evaporates as they are used – as glue sets, for instance. The kids could as easily be sniffing paint, nail-varnish remover, petrol, dry-cleaning fluid, degreasing compounds – or even more dangerously, aerosols. Some do, in fact, but glue, easily identifiable and readily available, caught on.

Inhaling solvents can produce sensations varying from light-headedness to nausea, disorientation, loss of control and hallucinogenic states (though the glue-sniffer's 'visions' are not true hallucinations, as they are rarely confused with reality).

The experience is like being drunk. Sniffing is generally a group activity and there is a lot of fooling about. The solvent takes effect almost instantaneously and wears off within half an hour of sniffing being stopped.

The hazards have been widely-publicised. A number of young people – a typical glue sniffer is in her or (more usually) his early teens – have died. The dangers fall into different categories: as a result of accidents when 'intoxicated'; choking on vomit after loss of consciousness; suffocation because of the method used (a plastic bag over the head or sniffing in a confined place), and heart failure due to dangerous substances entering the body.

All solvents are dangerous, but some are more dangerous than others. Sniffing directly from an aerosol can, for instance, mean the contents being inhaled as well as the vapours. Some forms of solvent abuse are believed to cause damage to kidneys, liver, lungs, bone marrow and skin. Different solvents carry different risks, and relatively little research has been done.

When someone is sniffing repeatedly the 'hangover' effect of pallor, tiredness, forgetfulness and loss of concentration can become a daily pattern. It is fairly easy to guess that someone has been sniffing glue from the strong smell on their breath, hair and clothing.

Physical dependence is not a real problem. Most sniffers will grow out of the habit – if, that is, their health is not damaged by it before that happens. A few may become psychologically dependent and become lone sniffers long after their friends have ceased.

At the moment of writing, it is not illegal to sell glue to minors. Many people would like to make it so. Others think that would be unworkable. Glue, after all, is only part of the problem. Would all products which contain solvents have to be banned? Where would you draw the line?

An alternative suggestion is to label certain products with health warnings. But, say the cynics, this would merely alert young people to alternatives they didn't know about. The most hopeful move is the introduction, by a major manufacturer, of 'sniff-proof' glue, a variety that has no intoxicating chemicals at all. It's one step towards the elimination of a particularly deadly craze.

Keith, a tall, good-looking boy, the eldest of 7 children. He started sniffing at 16 and, according to Bob was – 'Notorious, one of the worst sniffers in the area'.

'Everybody knew Keith. Nobody thought he would ever give up the habit.' He has, though, and so has his brother, though they still hang around with the glue-sniffing crowd from the council estate where they live. Keith talks ponderously, in a Black Country accent that at times has to be translated for my 'foreign' ears. Only when describing his hallucinations did he warm to the subject. His mother, Bob says, is a warm, caring woman, deeply attached to her eldest son, providing Keith with a background more secure than many of the boys in the group.

'I started sniffing when I was 16 and left school. I became a skinhead at the same time. It was just the thing to do then. There was a lot about it on the television. It was something new.

'I was the first around here. The others used to watch me at first, then they started too. For a while, after I came off this year, I felt a bit bad about that . . . wondering if I'd led them astray and that. Then I thought, well it's up to them isn't it? It's up to all of us what we do in the end. Nobody forced them.

'At first I was buying tubes, maybe two a day, then after a while it was tins. At the end, before I gave up, I was getting through two big tins a day. I had a job in a foundry for the first two years, then I found I couldn't sniff and work, so I gave up work. It was harder to buy the stuff with no wages; it took all my unemployment benefit. A big tin can cost £5. It was one of the reasons I stopped. Every penny I had was going on glue and there still wasn't enough.

'At first I used to sniff on my own – outside, in the street, anywhere. You see kids walking along in gangs now, with their glue bags, sniffing, but it was unusual four years ago. People used to look at me. I didn't care; that was part of it really – you knew they were talking about you, that they were shocked. You thought, "Well, I'm doing something they haven't the nerve to do." You felt different.

'The feeling is like being drunk, though I didn't know much about being drunk when I was sixteen. You just feel you don't care about anything. After a couple of months, I found I was having these dreams, hallucinations really. I could lie on the ground and look into the sky and a space invaders' game would appear. I could play space invaders in the sky. Other times it was a flying saucer or the clouds would turn into aeroplanes. You could see it exactly as if it was there – as real as pictures on a screen – but you knew it was a dream.

'If I looked at the traffic lights for a while, eagles would fly out of them. Say I'd been sniffing now, the characters on the wallpaper over there (The Mister Men) would come to life and jump down off the wallpaper. Usually you can decide what you want to see – those dreams, when they are good, are the best part of sniffing.

'You can have bad dreams though. With me it was spiders, great big, long-legged things. I'd be sitting somewhere, and suddenly I'd look down at the ground and they would be all around me, closing in. I'd close my eyes and cover my face and when I opened them, the spiders would have gone.

'My parents used to get fed up. My Dad never hit me because he hit me once and bruised me badly when I was little and he's never hit me since. Our Mom though – she would go on and on about how I was killing myself. It's a waste of time telling you that. Maybe it's true but it doesn't mean anything. Everything's bad for you – drink, cigarettes, sugar, salt. Glue is just another one for the list. If you listened to what people say you'd never do anything.

'I used to think a lot of my parents, particularly our Mom, but those years when I was sniffing killed it off. I don't care much what they think now. They chucked me out five times. I used to have to sleep in the garage. Me being the oldest, they were worried the others would copy me. My brother did, but he's given up now too, since he found himself a wench. Her Mom won't let her go out with him if he is still sniffing. He gave up his Mohican too. You have to have something to give up for – or a lot of will-power.

'My parents didn't even know for the first year I was sniffing. Then somebody told them and suddenly they started being able to smell it on my breath and being able to tell by my eyes. They might never have noticed if somebody hadn't said.

'I gave it up, like I said, because it was costing me too much and because there wasn't the kick in it there used to be. You just tell yourself you are not going to do it and that's it. It takes will power, that's all. In a way, I suppose I just grew out of it. There are lads older than me doing it, but it seems a bit stupid. It's for kids.

'I drink a bit now if I feel like it. Nobody minds that; nobody points a finger if you are drunk on alcohol. I'd like a job but there aren't any around now – four years ago, there were one or two if you were lucky. I still hang around with the sniffers because they are my mates. They are always laughing and fooling around. I know what they are feeling so it doesn't get on my nerves A lot of them will give up sniffing sooner or later; a few, I reckon, will be on it for life. No, I never try to get them to give up. I know they'd take as much notice as I did when people used to talk to me – none.'

Carl, small and scruffy and more than willing to chat. He is 19, and looks 16.

It is hard to believe he has just served four months for Grievous Bodily Harm. He lives alone ('Not really alone – I've got my dog') in a council flat. The flat is in a notorious block, accepted only as a last resort by those who are homeless and desperate. Because of his glue-sniffing, his father had thrown him out and he was sleeping rough.

'The first time I tried glue was when I was 15. A mate of mine had met this kid who was sniffing Evostick and he asked us if we wanted to have a go. We did and we liked it. From then on I spent all the money I could get on it and scrounged off mates who were sniffing when I was broke.

'At first I was only sniffing a couple of times a week. When I left school and went on a Youth Opportunities Scheme, I had a bit of money of my own, so I could buy some more glue. I suppose a tin would last me about three days.

'Usually though a few of us would share a tin, a group of lads. We'd go over the park at night and we'd all have a dollop of glue in an old bread bag or something. Sometimes we'd find an old house and we'd get in there and start a fire for warmth. It wasn't something I fancied on my own. It was like a night out, a whole gang of us having a laugh.

'A lot of the kids round here, the lads anyway, sniff. There's nothing else to do – no youth clubs or sports facilities and no jobs when you leave school. It means you've got a whole day and night with nothing to do. I think most of them start sniffing out of boredom.

'I was living with my Dad and my uncle and my handicapped older brother. My Mom left when I was little – she couldn't stand my Dad's drinking and the rows. I don't blame her now. I'd have liked to go and live with her – I hear from her sometimes – but she was made redundant from her job and couldn't have me.

'My Dad thought I was drinking at first because of the way I was acting. He didn't like that too much, but he might have put up with it. When I got picked up by the police for sniffing, that's when the trouble at home really started.

'He used to give me a good belting when I got home if he could smell glue off my breath. He threw me out a couple of times and I had to try and find a place to kip down. That made me sniff more. I was so miserable with nowhere to sleep that I'd buy or cadge some glue so I could forget about it for a while.

'My father said he would have me home as soon as I stopped sniffing and I tried. I'd come home, give it up for a while, then somebody would offer me some and I'd be off again. Once I managed to convince my father that I was off it for a long time. I'd chew packets of mints to hide the smell on my breath or have a pint of beer before I went home, and tell him I'd been out for a drink with my mates. When he found out the way I'd been pulling the wool over his eyes that time, he said he wouldn't have me back again.

'Two things made me give it up. One was the way sniffing changed my personality. I got violent. I hit one bloke just because he was staring at me and broke his nose. However high I was, I always knew what people were thinking: that you were a sniffer and the scum of the earth, and I couldn't take that. Then I got involved in the fight that put me inside.

'The other thing was that I started to get ill and it frightened me. I thought maybe I would die from sniffing like they say.

'It had got so that I spent most of the night sniffing and the whole of the next day sleeping it off. One day, a mate called and woke me up to help him move some furniture. I got up, but as I was walking down the road, I was like an old man. I could hardly breathe. I was wheezing and spitting phlegm and I nearly passed out. I thought "This is it – I'm going to die."

'I came off after that. I have a drink occasionally but not a lot. I may not be great, but I want to be myself. When you are sniffing, you become somebody else. Glue takes you over.

'I pick up my Giro every fortnight and I make sure I pay my rent. I take my dog for a walk and try to keep out of trouble. I see my father from time to time. We get on okay now. I can see why he acted like he did, why he got rid of me. It was the biggest favour he ever did me. It meant I got a place of my own and I had to stand on my own feet.'

For further information

55 Wood Street, Mitcham Junction, Surrey.
(Groups throughout the British Isles.)

DEPRESSION

The Samaritans, 17 Uxbridge Road, Slough
SLI ISN.
(National 24-hour telephone service 'For
those who are in despair or just need
someone to talk to.' Can put you in touch
with appropriate specialised help. The
telephone operator will put you through.)

DIET

Anorexic Aid, The Priory Centre, 11 Priory
Road, High Wycombe, Bucks.
(Regional self-help groups and newsletter.)

EDUCATION (FOR
PARENTS)

The Community Education Office, The
Open University, Walton Hall, Milton
Keynes, MK7 6AA.
(Runs a popular course called 'Parents and
Teenagers'.)
Exploring Parenthood, 54 Parkhill Road,
London NW3 2YP.
(Day and evening workshops for parents,
including some where teenagers are
encouraged to attend and discuss their
parent problems.)

EMPLOYMENT AND
UNEMPLOYMENT

*Careers and Occupational Information
Centre*, c/o Manpower Services
Commission, Moorfoot, Sheffield S1 4PQ.
(Leaflets and books aiming to help people
make informed decisions about jobs and
careers.)
Centres for the Unemployed, TUC,
Congress House, Great Russell Street,
London WC1B 3LS.
(Centres, country-wide, offering social and
educational activities.)

HOMOSEXUALITY

Parents Enquiry, 16 Henley Road, Catford,
London, SE6 2HZ.
(Advice, information and counselling for
young homosexuals and their families.
Country-wide counsellors.)

London Friend (Gay Counselling), 274
Upper Street, London N1 2UA.
(Support and information, including
whereabouts of local groups.)

ONE-PARENT
FAMILIES

Gingerbread, 35 Wellington Street, London
WC2.
National Council for One-Parent Families,
255 Kentish Town Road, London
NW5 2LX.

PARENTS UNDER
STRESS

Family Network, National Children's
Home, 85 Highbury Park, London
N5 1UD.
(Phone-in help/advice service. For nearest
number, see local press, telephone directory
or phone Organiser on 01 226 2033.)

PREGNANCY

LIFE, 7 Parade, Leamington Spa,
Warwickshire.
(Anti-abortion group, which provides help –
including accommodation if necessary – to
girls who want to have their babies.)
See also BIRTH CONTROL AND ABORTION.

YOUTH

National Youth Bureau, 17–23 Albion
Street, Leicester LE1 6GD.
(National resource centre for information,
publication, training, research and
development . . . everything you ever
wanted to know about young people in
society today. Incorporates The National
Association of Young People's Counselling
and Advisory Services, which can direct
young people to local counselling agencies.)

Books referred to in the text

Young People in the 80s, HMSO, London, 1983.

John Conger, *Adolescence – Generation under Pressure*, Harper & Row, New York, 1979.

James Hemming, *You and your Adolescent*, Ebury Press, London, 1975.

Irma Kurtz, *Crisis – A Guide to your Emotions*, Ebury Press, London, 1981.

Carol Lee, *The Ostrich Position*, Writers & Readers Cooperative Society in association with the Chameleon Editorial Group, 1983.

Brenda Maddox, *Step-parenting*, Unwin paperbacks, London, 1976.

Frank Musgrove, *Youth and Social Order*, Routledge & Kegan Paul, London, 1964.

Clare Rayner, *Related to Sex*, Paddington Press, London, 1979.

M. Rutter, 'Adolescent Turmoil – Fact or Fiction?' *Journal of Child Psychology*, Vol. 17, 1976.

Gail Sheehy, *Passages – Predictable Crises of Adult Life*, E. P. Dutton & Co., New York, 1976.

Miriam Stoppard, *Talking Sex*, Victor Gollancz, London, 1982.

Index